Listening to the evidence:
the future of UK resettlement

Conference proceedings

Victoria Park Plaza, London
6 February 2003

Edited by Verity Gelsthorpe and Lauren Herlitz

Further copies of this conference report are available from:
Communication Development Unit
Room 264
50, Queen Anne's Gate
London
SW1H 9AT

Tel: 020 7273 2084
fax: 020 7222 0211
email   publications.rds@homeoffice.gsi.gov.uk

This publication is also available on the RDS website:
Internet: http//www.homeoffice.gov.uk/rds/index.html

ISBN 1 84473 122 7

Contents

List of acronyms

AAPD	Asylum and Appeals Directorate
AIUK	Amnesty International UK
CD	Communications Directorate, Home Office
CIC	Citizenship and Immigration Canada
CRER	Centre for Research in Ethnic Relations, University of Warwick
CWS	Church World Service
DfES	Department for Education and Skills
DoH	Department of Health
DWP	Department for Work and Pensions
ECHR	European Convention on Human Rights
ECRE	European Councils on Refugees and Exiles
EECASS	East of England Consortium for Asylum Seeker Support
EMCASS	East Midlands Consortium for Asylum Seeker Support
FCO	Foreign and Commonwealth Office
HO	Home Office
HRA	Human Rights Act
IAA	Immigration Appellate Authority
IAPU	International Asylum Policy Unit, Home Office
IAS	Immigration Advisory Service
ICG	Immigration and Community Group, Research Development and Statistics Directorate, Home Office
ICMC	International Catholic Migration Commission

ICRC	International Committee of the Red Cross
IISS	International Institute for Strategic Studies
IND	Immigration and Nationality Directorate
INS	Immigration and Naturalisation Service, US
IOM	International Organization for Migration
IRC	International Rescue Committee
IRSS	Immigration Research and Statistics Service, Home Office
IS	Immigration Service
JAD	Jobseekers Analysis Division, Jobcentre Plus
LCD	Lord Chancellor's Department
LSC	Legal Services Commission
MPI	Migration Policy Institute, Washington D.C.
MSF	Médecins Sans Frontières
NASS	National Asylum Support Service
NECASS	North East Consortium for Asylum Support Services
NGO	Non Governmental Organisation
NWC	North West Consortium
ODPM	Office of the Deputy Prime Minister
OPE	Overseas Processing Entity
RA	Refugee Action
RAP	Refugee Arrivals Project
RC	Refugee Council
RSD	Refugee Status Determination
RDS	Research Development and Statistics Directorate, Home Office
RIU	Refugee Integration Unit, Home Office
RLC	Refugee Legal Centre

RSC	Refugee Studies Centre, University of Oxford
SASC	Scottish Asylum Seekers Consortium
SRC	Scottish Refugee Council
UNDP	United Nations Development Programme
UNHCR	United Nations High Commission(er) for Refugees
VMHS	Vietnamese Mental Health Service
WRAPS	Worldwide Refugee Applicant Processing System
WUS	World University Service
Y&H	Yorkshire and Humberside Consortium

Acknowledgements

This event was organised with the support and assistance of many people who enabled it to take place successfully within a very short time frame. We would especially like to thank those who kindly agreed to present papers and act as panel members: Vaughan Robinson, Sead Masic, Ruben Ahlvin, Erik Stenström, Joanne van Selm, Gil Loescher, and James Milner. Equally, we wish to thank all participants who gave up their time to take part in the event and share with us their experience, knowledge and suggestions about resettlement. Our thanks also go to Felicity Clarkson for rigorously chairing the event, and to Frank Laczko and Aikko Kikkawa from the International Organization of Migration (IOM) for preparing one of the background papers.

The overall co-ordination of the event was the responsibility of Verity Gelsthorpe from the Immigration Research and Statistics Service (IRSS), who together with Claire Downie from the Asylum and Appeals Policy Directorate (AAPD) conceptualised the seminar and this proceedings document. The contribution of Lauren Herlitz to the organisation of the event and this document was also invaluable. A number of staff within IRSS additionally played a key role in the organisation of the seminar and the smooth-running of the day itself, especially Beverley Martin-Mayo, Ralph Clarkson and Lesley Duff. Their input was greatly appreciated. Thank you also to all the workshop facilitators, including Jon Williams (AAPD), Penny Hart (AAPD), and Carolyne Tah (IRSS). Finally, this paper would not have been completed without the help of Mac Head (RDS) and Neil Moran (RDS) for their skilled Desk Top Publishing work.

IRSS
October 2003

Introduction

We are pleased to introduce the proceedings of the research conference, *Listening to the evidence: the future of UK resettlement,* which the Home Office Immigration Research and Statistics Service (IRSS) held on 6 February 2003. The conference brought together experienced resettlement practitioners, refugee community organisations of previously resettled refugees, academic experts, researchers, and policy makers from the Home Office and other Government Departments to discuss research and best practice on resettlement.

The aims of the conference were to:

- inform current policy development and implementation of the forthcoming UK resettlement programme; and
- inform future strategic policy development of the UK resettlement programme.

Specifically, the conference provided the opportunity for participants to:

- share existing research evidence, knowledge, experience, ideas, and examples of good practice on resettlement;
- consider lessons learned from past UK experience of *ad hoc* resettlement programmes; and
- identify the gaps in current knowledge and research evidence.

The conference was opened by Felicity Clarkson, Director of the Home Office Asylum and Appeals Policy Directorate. Presentations considering best practice from previous and existing resettlement programmes in the UK and elsewhere were given by academic experts from the field of resettlement, a representative from a refugee community organisation, and resettlement practitioners in Sweden. Participants had the opportunity to consider the content of the presentations and discuss their own knowledge and experiences of the resettlement process in morning and afternoon workshops. The conference was concluded by a plenary session, where participants could put their questions to the speakers and to policy officials.

Open and welcome
Felicity Clarkson, Director, Asylum and Appeals Policy Directorate (AAPD), Home Office

A very warm welcome here to our conference on resettlement. Many thanks to those of you who have come quite a long way to help us prepare, in a sense, for a journey of our own on resettlement. I am sure we are going to have a very interesting and stimulating day.

Today, we are bringing together a wide range of people who are or have been involved in resettlement programmes, to teach us in the Home Office and in the refugee community in the UK how to go about it. We do not think that we can do it without the help and expertise of those who have been through this journey before. Although the UK has undertaken some resettlement with particular individuals, we still have a great deal more to learn. Feel free to tell us, I hope in a constructive spirit, what has worked and what did not, what the barriers were, and how things could have worked better.

The Home Secretary has a firm intention and belief that the UK should offer greater opportunities for a 'durable solution' for those really in need of protection. I am asked why we have pitched it at five hundred. I felt that it was a number that could be managed. It is also about succeeding and affordability when we start, and we do not want to set ourselves up to fail. That would be a bad experience for everybody. But the Home Secretary will be impatient from the outset for greater numbers, because, as I say, he sees very strongly that this is part of the UK's positive response to the needs of refugees.

In the spirit of wanting to start and succeed, we have decided to start with as straightforward an approach as we believe is possible in a complicated world, because we know that our processes will need time to bed down and to iron out 'wrinkles'. Our proposals at the moment are with the Home Secretary. Our current ideas are set out in the background papers and I think you will agree that the papers circulated for this conference are very comprehensive, so there is no need to go into much detail here. It is likely that to start with we will focus on only one or two regions in the world, well beyond the UK. In essence, the Home Office will have oversight of the programme, and aims to fund a large proportion of the costs involved. Our initial view is that funding or support will continue beyond the initial reception period up to a maximum of a year, after which we hope that refugees will either be self-supporting or will revert to general state benefits. There are representatives from the other Departments that we are working with here today, so welcome to them.

Please take the opportunity to meet with the team working on resettlement. For the benefit of our speakers and for our audience, please be reassured that we are among friends here. This is an occasion to help us along the way. I am sure we will have a very constructive day's discussion.

Thank you.

Presentations

Listening to the evidence: the future of UK resettlement

1.

Vaughan Robinson, Professor, University of Wales, Swansea

Prof. Vaughan Robinson studied at Oxford University where he took his first degree and his doctorate. He then became a Prize Research Fellow at Nuffield College Oxford before moving to University of Wales, Swansea in 1982. He founded the Migration Unit at University of Wales, Swansea in 1992, which he now directs. Vaughan is author or editor of eight books on migration, refugees and asylum seekers, including on previous country specific resettlement programmes, most notably on the Vietnamese and Bosnians.

An evidence base for future policy: reviewing UK resettlement policy

Introduction

This paper reviews the academic literature which has described and evaluated the main programmes formulated by the UK government to resettle refugees in the post-war period. This review will provide some historical context for the formulation of the new resettlement programme that is due to be implemented in Summer 2003, and also seek to identify any common principles that have underlain past programmes, highlighting key factors that have led to the 'success' and 'failure' of previous programmes.

Although over fifty pieces of literature have been reviewed for this chapter it should be noted that there is not really a full or comprehensive evidence-base upon which the new programme can be based. This is because much of the extant literature suffers from two problems. It either reports the findings of very localised research that may not be generalisable to the whole country, or it simply describes national programmes rather than evaluates them. Nevertheless, despite the fact that the evidence-base is far from perfect, it is still possible to learn something of value from past resettlement programmes.

Past resettlement programmes

Six government programmes will be reviewed in chronological order, namely those to resettle Polish ex-servicemen, Ugandan Asian expellees, Chilean dissidents, Vietnamese quota refugees, Bosnian evacuees, and Kosovan evacuees. Technically the last two of these programmes should not be included in a review of 'resettlement' programmes, since they sought to provide only temporary protection for groups who it was assumed would quickly return to their home countries when the ethnic cleansing, which had prompted their flight, ended. The programmes therefore focused on short-term goals rather than upon long-term settlement and integration. Despite this difference of emphasis, the way in which these two programmes were devised and implemented bears a striking similarity to the other four programmes and lessons can be learned from their successes and failures which are of value to contemporary decision makers.

The discussion of each of the six programmes will be structured in the same way. First an account will be provided of the contextual and programme-specific factors that policy-makers had to take into account when formulating policy. Then the programme will be described, along with how it was implemented. Lastly, the policy outcomes will be outlined and the programme evaluated. A final summary section will draw together all of the separate discussions of the six programmes and an attempt will be made to indicate what have been the successful elements of past programmes and what have been the unsuccessful ones.

The Polish programme, 1945-49 on

Policy considerations

After the end of the Second World War the UK government was faced with the task of resettling around 300,000 Polish exiles who had either fled to Britain during the war (Sword, Davies & Ciechanowski, 1989) or had been accepted as stateless European Volunteer Workers immediately after the war (Tannahill, 1958). This community was unable to return to its home country because the Yalta conference had put Poland behind the Iron Curtain.

The key factors which bore on government decision-making were:

- The majority of the Poles were military personnel who were young, mainly single men. They had not been selected by the government for settlement but had selected themselves by spontaneous flight.
- They constituted men who were disaffected with the outcome of the war and were still armed. The Foreign Office therefore wanted to 'civilianise' them as quickly as possible to neutralise any threat which they might pose to national security and civil order.
- They were already dispersed in clusters around the UK in the military barracks which had accommodated them during the war.
- They had refused to accept the legitimacy of the Nazi-supported wartime government in Poland and had therefore created their own government-in-exile in London, along with a Polish Cultural Centre in Hammersmith which had its own library and university courses.
- They had already established their own religious institutions, having recruited peripatetic Polish clerics to provide catholic services around the UK. And they had formed the SPK, a cultural organisation committed to maintaining the Polish language and reinstating democracy in Poland.

The Poles were thus a highly organised and institutionally complete community which had its own internal power structure and resources.

On a different level, the government had to take account of the fact that the country was facing an acute housing shortage arising from wartime bombing, and that the popular mood in the immediate post-war period had become xenophobic. There was thus resistance in some areas to the settlement of the Poles, and the National Union of Mineworkers, for example, waged a strenuous campaign to deny Poles the opportunity of working in the coalmines. However, none of this negated the fact that the Poles, because of their demography, represented a considerable resource in a country where sectoral labour shortages were hampering post-war reconstruction.

Policy implementation

The government opted for an unusual way of resettling the Poles. Rather than demilitarise them and then make their resettlement the responsibility either of the Ministry of Labour, the Home Office or the Foreign Office, it was decided to create the Polish Resettlement Corp (PRC). This was a non-operational unit of the British Army that was funded directly by the War Office. Enlistment was voluntary but those Poles who did enlist were guaranteed a salary, free accommodation and help in finding work, so few declined the opportunity. For the government, delegation offered clear benefits: the Poles were effectively responsible for their own resettlement within the confines of principles laid down by government departments; the Poles remained subject to military law; and the threat to national security could therefore be contained (Sword, Davies & Ciechanowski, 1989).

Two hundred and sixty-five military camps were handed over to the PRC to house the Poles and it was acknowledged and accepted that resettlement would take several years and that the camps would therefore become Accommodation Centres not Reception or Transit Centres. Camps were used because of the shortage of housing in the private and public sectors and also because it was felt that uncomfortable accommodation might encourage some Poles to seek onward migration to the US or Canada. The camps were deliberately dispersed across the UK at the request of the Foreign Office, which feared that disaffected young soldiers might quickly resort to mass disobedience if the programme did not go well.

The key goal of the programme was to get the Poles into jobs, not only to ensure their economic self-sufficiency, but also to begin the process of integration. Accommodation was thought to be much less important and there is evidence that some Poles lived in the camps for extended periods after they acquired their first job. The camps therefore became industrial dormitories as well as Accommodation Centres, with Poles being channelled into particular industries that had acute labour shortages (e.g. agriculture, the steel industry and the coal industry). When individuals were ready to leave the camps they found their own accommodation in the wider community, with most following the then common route for working people of renting rooms near to where they worked (Sword, Davies & Ciechanowski, 1989).

The funding of the programme followed a model that has since been termed 'front-end loading' in which resources were allocated mainly to the 'reception' phase, with integration costs being picked up either by local authorities or through block funding of mainstream expenditure.

Policy outcomes

There has been little evaluation of the Polish programme but the accounts which do exist allow us to piece together some of the key outcomes. Most Poles found work near to the camp within which they were billeted, so that the initial administrative decision to disperse the Poles produced a dispersed settlement pattern. Many Poles were understandably keen to remain within localities and communities with which they had become familiar while living in the camps. Hence the 1951 Census records Polish-born communities in remote counties such as Merioneth, Anglesey, Northumberland and Cornwall. Equally, though, the attraction of the community that had formed during the war in London and its associated institutions and facilities encouraged some secondary migration of Poles from the regions to the capital (Zubrzycki, 1956). As a result, by 1951, London and Middlesex contained one-third of the nation's Polish-born population.

Partly as a result of the resettlement strategy, Polish communities quickly developed throughout the UK, each with its own branch of the SPK, its own Polish club and its own Polish-language church services. At a national level, the organised nature of the Polish community and their determination to keep alive the idea of a free Poland ensured that the community institutions which they had created during the war were maintained, even strengthened. Polish language newspapers were published in the UK and the Cultural Centre still exists, as did, until recently, a Polish hospital in North Wales and a Polish retirement home in Devon.

Patterson's studies of the Polish community in the 1960s and 1970s describe a well-integrated population that has inter married with the indigenous population and gained steady occupational mobility matched by commensurate social and residential mobility (Patterson, 1977).

The Ugandan Asian programme, 1972-73

Policy considerations

The Ugandan Asians were very different to the Poles, and policy had to be formulated in a different political and social context, as the following discussion illustrates.

Britain agreed to resettle 28,600 of the 80,000 Ugandan Asians expelled by President Amin in Autumn 1972 (Marett, 1989; Robinson, 1995), but the government was given only 90 days to prepare a reception and resettlement programme because of the peremptory way in which the expulsion was announced. In addition, the Ugandan Asians were a visible minority arriving in the UK after large-scale black and Asian migration had racialised the immigration issue in the minds of the British public. Kohler (1973), for example, demonstrated how 57 per cent of a national sample were against admitting the Ugandan Asians, and Bristow (1976) and Marett (1993) have described how there was resistance in some quarters and localities to their resettlement. The National Front was also ready to make political capital out of any signs of generosity towards the new arrivals.

Set against these difficulties was the fact that many of the Ugandan Asians had been successful businessmen who had, as a community, appreciated the value of education and qualifications. Moreover, many were already fluent in spoken and written English and they arrived in the UK as permanent settlers without a 'Myth of Return' (Robinson, 1986). Many were Gujurati Hindus and, as part of that diaspora, already knew or were related to Gujurati Hindus living in long-established communities in UK cities such as Leicester. And they came largely as families rather than as single people.

The arrival of the Ugandan Asians was sympathetically covered by the national print media, which played up the middle-class background of many of the refugees, their treatment in Uganda, and the despotic nature of Amin's rule.

Policy implementation

The government again delegated reception and resettlement to a 'quango', in this case the Uganda Resettlement Board. This body was given the job of establishing policy and overseeing its implementation, and it was given a budget of £6.1 million to achieve this. The actual day-to-day implementation of policy was then further delegated to a range of charities (e.g. the Red Cross) which had agreed to provide services (Swinerton *et al*, 1975). And in turn, these charities expected considerable assistance from active citizens who were prepared to volunteer their time to work in centres.

Sixteen military camps were requisitioned to provide Reception Centres, and these were distributed across the UK, although this dispersed pattern of provision arose more from availability than from any considered decision. The camps were never intended as Accommodation Centres, but simply holding centres to allow people to be processed and matched to permanent accommodation.

The government again opted for front-end loading and the mainstreaming of longer-term service provision, and initially, at least, local authorities were not reimbursed for additional expenditure arising from accepting refugees. Only after sustained pressure did they agree to adjust the Rate Support Grant to compensate authorities. The

Ugandan Asians therefore received no special educational or training provision, nor did the government agree to provide preferential loans for those entrepreneurs keen to return to business, but lacking start-up funding.

However, the Ugandan Asian programme marked an evolution of policy in two important ways. First, the main objective of resettlement policy was no longer to find work for refugees, but to ensure that they acquired mainstream housing in the community as quickly as possible, thereby forestalling any institutionalisation that could be induced by extended living in camps. This housing was to be acquired by asking local authorities to volunteer vacant stock. Second, the Ugandan Asians were to have their settlement patterns engineered through direct state intervention. The government was keen to avoid ghettoisation of the new arrivals and therefore proposed a dispersal policy that was actioned through the declaration of 'Red' (or No go) areas and 'Green' (or Go) areas. Red areas were supposed to be areas of housing stress but were, according to some commentators, simply areas which already housed sizeable Asian populations (Evans, 1972; Dines, 1973; Ward, 1973). However, Ugandan Asians were to be allowed to decide whether they wished to be dispersed or whether they preferred to find their own accommodation.

Policy outcomes

Initially the programme was hamstrung by the failure of local authorities to volunteer accommodation, and it was only when £2 million (Marett, 1989) was added to the Rate Support Grant of authorities willing to take refugees that housing became available in quantity. Also problematic was the fact that housing offers were heavily concentrated in the old industrial conurbations, many of which already had ethnic populations. The government was unwilling to requisition housing or use its own housing stock.

Dispersed resettlement was also made difficult by three factors. First, the perceptions that Ugandan Asians held of the UK. Most knew only the cities of London and Leicester and were not inclined to accept accommodation elsewhere. Bristow (1976) thus found that only 38 per cent of all arrivals eventually accepted offers of government accommodation, with the remainder moving to accommodation that they, or their relatives, had found in the south-east and east Midlands (Robinson, 1986). Second, was the length of time that many Ugandan Asians had to wait in Reception Centres for offers of state accommodation: some 39 per cent of the total simply left the Centre within which they were living and found their own accommodation rather than wait any longer (Bristow, 1976). The third factor, was the poor orientation information that was provided for them in these centres.

Those who did accept the offer of state housing also often found themselves in locations that made integration difficult (Dines, 1973) and economic self-sufficiency even more difficult (Kumar, 1973).

In the short-term, these difficulties produced some secondary migration of those who had been dispersed (CRC 1974; CRC 1976) and some housing problems for those living with relatives or friends in Red areas. Overall, though, Adams and Bristow (1979) found the dispersed to be well-housed, with 73 per cent having been given council houses.

In the medium term, the Ugandan Asians have been a remarkable success story and have even been given the sobriquet 'model minority' by the popular press. They have achieved remarkable social mobility across the country (Robinson, 1993a; Robinson & Valeny, 2003), nowhere more so than in Leicester (Marett, 1993), a city they were advised to avoid when they first arrived (Marett, 1989).

The Chilean 'Programme', 1974-79

Policy considerations

Although there was never an official 'Chilean programme', the government did accept and resettle some 3,000 political exiles from the regime of General Pinochet between 1974 and 1979. There was a good deal of public support in the UK for these political refugees and this was manifested through the spontaneous formation of over forty local Chile Solidarity Campaigns in Britain and the actions of various trade unions which lobbied for the release of political prisoners (Kay, 1987). Many of the latter had been incarcerated for considerable periods of time and had also been tortured, and their release was only made possible by the intervention of international human rights organisations such as the United Nations (UN).

Also important was that the Chileans were not a visible minority and that many were well-educated, although few could speak English before coming to this country. Very few had elected to come to the UK as their first choice since there was little knowledge about Britain in that country and people naturally looked to the United States as their preferred destination. Rather, they were pre-selected by humanitarian organisations. Even those who were sponsored by British organisations such as the World University Service (WUS) were making a step into the unknown. Moreover, most wished actively to continue the struggle against Pinochet and, initially at least, intended to return home when his government had been overthrown. Integration was therefore far from their thoughts.

Policy implementation

There is very little literature on the policies that were introduced to resettle the Chileans. However it is known that in July 1974 a group of charities and activist groups combined their resources to form the Joint Working Group for Refugees from Chile (JWG). WUS continued to be responsible for the thousand or so Chileans who came to the UK to continue their education, and simply met them at Heathrow before escorting them to the University that had offered them a place. The remainder were met by the staff of the JWG, who took them to a Reception Centre in London that had been funded by an initial grant from the Home Office and which was then funded by a rolling programme of recurrent grants. They stayed there four weeks, during which time they received medical assistance, counselling, and orientation classes. When they left the Centre, they were handed over to one of the eight regional co-ordinators who oversaw all aspects of resettlement and were funded by the charities.

The government again refused to countenance targeted service provision. Front-end loading meant that again, reception was funded centrally, but resettlement and integration were not. Local authorities that volunteered to accept Chileans were not reimbursed (Browne, 1979). The government again decided that accommodation should take precedence over employment, but that housing should not be requisitioned, built or bought, but should be volunteered by those authorities with the political will to do so (Joly, 1987).

Policy outcomes

Because local authorities knew that they would receive no financial help if they resettled Chileans, offers were slow to materialise, and tended to come from areas where authorities had been lobbied by local labour groups or support groups. As a result, offers were concentrated in the older industrial cities of the north, Scotland or the Midlands, and the Chileans found themselves being denied the opportunity to live in the south-east. Kay (1987) argues that this dispersal took place against the wishes of the Chileans and actively disempowered them.

Furthermore, the dispersed Chileans were often sent to areas which lacked the infrastructure and experience to support minorities who did not speak English as their first language. Many Chileans found themselves living in cities where there were few other Spanish-speakers and where local authorities had failed to provide language classes. The latter situation was not helped by an eighteen-month-long argument between the Home Office and the Department of Education about who should fund language classes (Browne, 1979).

The inadequate provision of language tuition was not the only problem. The local authorities which offered housing were often unfamiliar with refugees, their needs and their entitlements. This became a major issue for those who had experienced torture, but was also a significant problem for all Chileans, only 50 per cent of whom ever received any employment training (Browne, 1979).

The sense of isolation that gripped some Chileans stimulated their secondary migration to London (Levin, 1981). This migration augmented a Chilean community that had begun to develop in the capital when the JWG found itself so short of accommodation in the regions that it had to accept and use offers of local authority housing in London. In fact, 31 per cent of all Chileans were eventually resettled by the JWG in London.

The Vietnamese Programme, 1979-82

Policy Considerations

Britain's involvement in the Vietnamese refugee crisis was part of an international burden-sharing agreement. The UK accepted two quotas of Vietnamese refugees totalling 11,450 people (Robinson, 1993b), to which a further 3,150 people were later added as a result of rescues at sea, and a final 3,850 people were added as part of a family reunion programme. Most of Britain's Vietnamese came from the closed or open refugee camps in Hong Kong.

The demographics of the group were highly skewed. They were very youthful and were predominantly ethnic Chinese from the north of the country (Jones, 1983). The Home Affairs Select Committee (1985) claimed that because Britain's selection criteria had been less stringent than those of the US or Australia, the Vietnamese who came to the UK were largely uneducated, illiterate even in their own language, possessing few transferable skills, and with little previous contact with western cultures.

The Vietnamese who came to the UK could not rely upon help from a pre-existing ethnic community here since the UK had never been a traditional destination for Vietnamese international migrants. Moreover they were a visible minority that arrived during a period when the National Front attracted over 191,000 votes in the 1979 General Election and Britain experienced the worst urban 'race riots' it had ever seen.

The media did, however, report very positively on the plight of the 'Boat People', and raised awareness of the harrowing circumstances of their flight from Vietnam. Consequently, there was at least initial public support for their settlement in the UK.

Policy implementation

The Vietnamese programme was clearly modelled on the earlier Ugandan Asian programme (see Robinson, 1985). Again, the government front-end loaded funding to the reception phase. Overall responsibility was delegated to a new body, the Joint Committee for Refugees from Vietnam (JCRV), which had the task of selecting refugees, controlling the rate of their arrival, and overseeing their settlement in this country. Reception was then further delegated to nominated charities, each of which was given its own geographical territory. The charities opened some 46 Reception Centres (with 3,800 bedspaces), many of which were located in old military bases (JCRV, 1982). Their geographical distribution was driven by the availability of suitable buildings, and the Centres were highly geographically dispersed because of this. Refugees were expected to remain in the Centres for a maximum of three months, during which time they would receive language tuition and orientation classes (Hale, 1993).

Local authorities were again asked to volunteer suitable housing, and getting people into permanent accommodation was the key goal of policy. Authorities were also expected to take responsibility for resettlement but they were not initially directly reimbursed for this commitment or for any housing they might offer. Instead, the Vietnamese were to be supported through mainstream provision and by local volunteer support groups which acted as links between refugees and local society and institutions.

Finally, the Vietnamese programme marked the introduction of compulsory, no-choice dispersal. Vietnamese were to be scattered across the whole of the UK (including rural areas and Northern Ireland) in small groups of 4-10 families (Robinson, 1993b). This was designed to 'spread the burden' (Home Affairs Select Committee, 1985), make it easier to acquire accommodation (Jones, 1982), aid integration (Jones, 1982), prevent ghettoisation (Robinson, 1993b), and prevent the local support groups from being overwhelmed (JCRV, 1982).

Policy outcomes

Whilst the Vietnamese programme did resettle a large number of refugees within a short period of time and in such a way as not to provide political capital for the extreme right, it had four fatal flaws and a series of other weaknesses.

First, the suitability of settlement areas was never rigorously vetted. There is no evidence that the JCRV ever had any criteria against which the suitability of settlement locations could be compared (Edholm, Roberts and Sayer, 1983). Instead, they were prepared to consider any offers of accommodation, no matter where they were located. Also, as shortages of housing offers meant refugees were having to remain longer and longer in Reception Centres, the JCRV increasingly used whatever accommodation was offered it. This meant that Vietnamese were dispersed to inappropriate areas where they had no access to suitable employment, education or language classes (JCRV, 1982). Nor was there any matching of families to areas, with, for example, a skilled boat-builder being settled in Birmingham.

Second, the programme dispersed the Vietnamese too thinly across the UK. They were dispersed in such small numbers that they were denied the opportunity to create their own communities (Somerset, 1983) and to look to these for support (JCRV, 1982). And their scattered settlement pattern meant that there was such a small number of people in any one locality that few local authorities felt it worthwhile to provide specialist services (Edholm, Roberts and Sayer, 1983).

Third, dispersal was undermined by the reliance upon voluntary offers of housing. Although it had set itself the goal of dispersal, the JCRV never acquired the powers to ensure that it could achieve this. Instead, the pattern of settlement was driven by the location of housing offers. As a result, significant concentrations of Vietnamese were allowed to develop in London, Birmingham, and Bristol (Robinson and Hale, 1989).

Fourth, the government never considered how the Vietnamese would react to being settled in inappropriate locations when they later acquired the freedom to move.

Once Vietnamese had been dispersed, little formal effort was made to anchor them in their new homes. Instead, isolation and the desire to live near friends, family, and co-ethnics prompted widespread secondary migration from rural and remote areas (Robinson and Hale, 1989). People moved to London, Birmingham, and Manchester, where they formed viable ethnic communities that became institutionally complete. In these cities they clustered in particular neighbourhoods and wards, often initially stopping with relatives or friends in overcrowded accommodation (Robinson, 1993c).

Critics have also pointed to other weaknesses in the Vietnamese programme beyond these four major issues. The Reception Centres were thought to have been problematic in two ways: some were so large that they became proto-communities that people did not want to leave (JCRV, 1982); and few provided adequate orientation information to allow Vietnamese to make informed choices about their futures. The Volunteer Support Groups were thought to have been a good idea, but some of the Groups felt that too much had been asked of them (Jones, 1983), that they had been inadequately resourced, and that their contribution had been undervalued (Robinson, 1993c).

The Bosnia Programme, 1992-95

Policy considerations

Britain accepted two quotas of Bosnian ex-detainees and their families in November 1992 and August 1995. Not all those offered temporary asylum took the opportunity and eventually only 2,585 people arrived in the UK, the majority of whom were young single males from rural communities. Most possessed few formal qualifications (Robinson and Coleman, 2000).

The Bosnians arrived in the UK with little advance warning, although the press had generally been sympathetic to their plight and had reported extensively on conditions in the camps in Bosnia. The Bosnians were also not a visible minority, and were not expected to remain in the UK. Most initially claimed that they wished to return to their homeland once conditions improved, and this orientation to temporary exile certainly impacted upon how they integrated in the UK. There was also no pre-existing Bosnian community in the UK to which the new arrivals could turn for help or support.

Policy implementation

The Bosnian programme was devised in great haste. Central government established general principles for the programme but then delegated implementation to the Refugee Council and the British Red Cross (Robinson and Coleman, 2000). Key amongst these principles were that Bosnians should remain in Reception Centres only for a limited time, that they should be dispersed across the country in clusters and definitely not in London, that they should not be resettled in areas of housing stress, that they should not be able to access housing through the homelessness legislation, and that local authorities should, yet again, be asked to volunteer accommodation.

Initially the Bosnians were to be dispersed widely, like the Vietnamese. However, under pressure from the Refugee Council, the government eventually agreed to a policy of clustered dispersal with refugees being settled in six clusters that were distributed across the UK.

Reception Centres were run by the charities and Bosnians were expected to spend no more than a month in such institutions. They were then to be channelled to one of the six cluster areas each of which was twinned with a Centre.

Unlike previous programmes, successful resettlement was defined much more broadly than the simple provision of housing, and a range of integration needs were to be taken into account when resettlement zones were being selected. Cluster areas had to offer appropriate healthcare, education, employment, training, language support, and to have tolerant and accepting local populations.

The new programme also took much more seriously the need to create and anchor communities. Mid-Term Support Teams were established in each of the cluster areas to offer advice and assistance, and each cluster area also had its own Development Worker whose remit was to assist with the formation of self-sustaining communities.

Policy outcomes

The government made it difficult to meet one of its own objectives by allowing one of the Reception Centres to be located in London. This made it virtually impossible to avoid Bosnian settlement in London. Eventually, the government allow some Bosnians to remain in the capital. In addition, the very different philosophies and practices of the charities entrusted with implementing policy ensured that some Bosnians were given more choice over where they could settle than others. Some were offered only one destination, as the government had stipulated, but others were offered three or more destinations (Robinson and Coleman, 2000).

Despite this, 90 per cent of all Bosnians were successfully resettled in the six cluster areas, which varied in size from 185 persons to 700 persons (Robinson and Coleman, 2000). The activities of the Community Development Workers also nurtured the formation of communities and community associations in each of the cluster areas, and these successfully anchored people in the places to which they had been sent. The Refugee Council estimated that fewer than 200 Bosnians had engaged in secondary migration by 1997, and Robinson and Coleman (2000) found mobility rates of less than seven per cent in the West Yorkshire cluster area, with most moves being made simply to access better housing. The Development Workers also liaised with service providers to raise their awareness of the Bosnians and their needs, to encourage open access to existing services, and to stimulate the provision of new services.

The Mid-Term Support Teams were also valued. They offered advice and translating and interpreting services, and effectively formed a professionalised version of the Vietnamese local Volunteer Support Groups or a precursor to the contemporary One-Stop Advice Centres.

The Kosovan Programme, 1999

Policy considerations

Very little literature exists on the Kosovan programme and those who were involved in it feel that the lessons which were learned have yet to be adequately recorded for posterity. The Home Office's own evaluation of the programme largely assesses the effectiveness of the management structures that were used rather than how the policies themselves actually worked (Compass Partnership, 2000).

It is known that the UK government responded in 1999 to requests from United Nations High Commissioner for Refugees (UNHCR) to give temporary sanctuary to a quota of Kosovan refugees from the camps on the Macedonian/Kosovan border. The first evacuees flew into the country on 25 April, and by the time the evacuation was halted on 25 June, Britain had received 4,346 Kosovans. They were expected to remain in the country for only a short period of time and the programme therefore deliberately never addressed long-term resettlement and integration issues.

The media in the UK was very positive about the plight of the Kosovans, and extensively covered the ethnic cleansing that had led to their flight. Gibney (1999) regards this positive media coverage as being vital to the success of the programme and the acceptance of the Kosovans by the British public. Nevertheless, this positive portrayal of the Kosovans has to be set against declining general support for admitting asylum seekers into the country, and the problematisation and racialisation of asylum seekers.

Policy implementation

The £13.7 million programme had two phases. In the first, which ran from April until early May, the government turned to four charities and delegated reception and resettlement to them. The Refugee Council, Refugee Action, the British Red Cross, and the Scottish Refugee Council were each given control of a specific geographical region, which then became *de facto* cluster areas. The charities co-ordinated their actions through the Inter-agency Management Group (IaMG). Their Arrivals Team met refugees at the airport, took them through immigration, fed them, provided them with any necessary medical treatment and then took them to the Reception Centre. Eight Reception Centres were opened, with four of these being located in Scotland, two in Leeds, one in Derbyshire, and one in Leicester. These dealt with all aspects of evacuees' needs following their arrival in the UK.

A second phase of the programme was prompted by the government's decision to increase sharply the size of the intake. Estimates of the total intake rose to 20,000 and the programme had therefore to be moved onto a different footing. The IaMG gave responsibility for this phase to local authorities, and the charities became specialist consultants and advisors to the authorities, who acted as providers. Local authorities therefore opened and managed 42 Reception Centres around the UK, and these eventually serviced 85 per cent of the total intake. Local authorities were expected to rehouse Kosovans from these Centres by allocating them vacant social housing in the vicinity or acquiring stock from local Housing Associations.

Policy outcomes

The Kosovan Programme has been so poorly documented by academics that it is difficult to know what the outcomes were. The general feeling seems to be that the Programme was a 'success' but it is difficult to know against what criteria commentators are judging success or failure.

We do know that evacuees were initially rehoused speedily from the Reception Centres. With the ending of the war in Kosovo on 25 June 1999, the evacuation was terminated abruptly. Whereas initially there was intense pressure to move people on quickly from the Reception Centres into more permanent accommodation, so as to free up bedspaces in the Centres for new arrivals, the ending of the war took away this immediate pressure. However, whilst the local authorities did not seem averse to using the Reception Centres to provide relatively permanent accommodation, the charities felt that this was unwise. They argued that lengthy stays in Centres would lead to the progressive institutionalisation of the Kosovans. They therefore pressured the local authorities to move people into mainstream accommodation and close the Centres. Compass notes that this had not been entirely successful, since by 25 April 2000 (i.e. one year after arrival) some 952 refugees still remained in local authority Reception Centres. In cases where people were moved on from Reception Centres, local authorities found them alternative accommodation. In Leicester, for example, the City Council provided housing for all those 124 people moving out of the Cygnet Hotel Reception Centre, and in Derbyshire all the Kosovans were housed by Derby City Council in the same neighbourhood of the city.

Analysis of the Compass Partnership report shows that a clear effort was made to cluster the Kosovans, although no information is provided that might allow us to see whether this was deliberate policy or an accident of where Reception Centres were available. Compass indicates that about 1,700 Kosovans were 'dispersed' to the north-west, c1,600 to Yorkshire and Humberside, and c380 to Scotland. Thus fully 85 per cent of all arrivals were dispersed to the three main cluster areas. They also note that about 380 Kosovans were resettled in the south-east. The report also mentions a cluster in the east Midlands but provides no statistics for this area.

The evolution of policy: key principles

The brief literature review above allows us to identify the key principles which have, over time, come to underpin and inform British refugee resettlement policy. These are as follows:

- Policy has been based upon the assumption that since immigration is a national issue, all parts of the country should contribute to its resolution. London and the south-east should not have to shoulder a disproportionate share of the costs simply because they are geographically close to the main ports of entry and are popular with refugees.
- The state has never believed in strong central government control in relation to resettlement. Rather it has preferred to delegate responsibility for reception and resettlement to NGOs and rely upon the help of active citizens. It has also chosen never to use its legal powers to requisition housing or force local authorities to take quotas of refugees against their wishes.
- The state has, for some time, had a clear vision of what constitutes a desirable geographical pattern of refugee settlement, even if it has failed to ensure that it has the necessary powers and mechanisms in place to achieve this vision.
- Successive governments have tended to spend more on receiving quota refugees than resettling them in the longer term.
- Governments have preferred to mainstream welfare support for quota refugees rather than risk being criticised for giving one vulnerable group extra help, possibly at the expense of others.
- Over time, governments have realised the importance of integrating refugees and have broadened their definition of successful resettlement accordingly.
- Over time, governments have begun to appreciate the importance of anchoring quota refugees in self-sustaining and well-supported communities, and have recognised that without such community development work refugees will simply leave the areas to which they have been dispersed.

What worked?

This concluding section attempts to summarise some of the lessons which can be learned from previous refugee resettlement programmes in the UK. It does so in three sub-sections, one of which considers reception policies and practice, the second of which considers geographical patterns of settlement, and the third of which looks at how support has been provided.

Reception strategies

The Vietnamese programme showed us clearly that the success of reception and resettlement begins with selection. While the prime selection criterion for quota refugees should be their need for protection, governments need to ensure that they do not simply pluck people from one form of vulnerability and place them in another. Many of the Vietnamese who came to Britain could not speak or understand English. As a result, when they were dispersed they became isolated, many suffered from depression, few could support themselves, there were reports of family tensions and marital breakdown, and many men simply retreated into themselves and remained within their homes.

Past resettlement programmes have demonstrated the importance of Reception Centres. Their size is important, since if they are too large they become communities to which people become attached. Where they are located is important. They need to be carefully sited, preferably within the resettlement zones that they will ultimately feed. Refugees inevitably become familiar with the area around their Reception Centre and can then be loath to leave this familiar environment. Reception Centres therefore need to be located in cities that offer long-term integration opportunities not just in places that can offer cheap vacant buildings. How long people remain in the Centres is important since prolonged residence can produce institutionalization and dependence.

The orientation classes offered in Centres are vital since they determine whether refugees can later make informed choices when offered alternative places of residence or training opportunities. Standardised, centrally-produced, and highly visual orientation material is needed. And Reception Centres can act as a vital bridge between reception and integration and between the newly-arrived and the resettled. Centres can become community resources and places of sanctuary for those who have been resettled and they can also act as conduits through which the resettled can pass their learning onto the newly-arrived.

Moreover, none of the above is negated even if the model that is adopted is a Reception Centre + Accommodation Centre model. The problems that the National Asylum Support Service (NASS) has had getting people to move out of emergency accommodation in London shows how quickly people can form bonds with a location.

Settlement geography

Settlement geography is also an important element within a successful resettlement programme. The literature shows that dispersal policies have largely failed, and in doing so have imposed huge personal, social and financial costs. In contrast, the clustering of the Bosnians was very successful.

However whilst clustering new arrivals is important in its own right, where these clusters are located is also highly significant. In the past, settlement geography has tended to be driven by the availability of cheap and vacant accommodation rather than by the needs of refugees or the conditions necessary for successful integration. There is no evidence that any UK programme has been based upon a thorough analysis of local labour market data, for instance, nor have there been well articulated mechanisms for feeding information about the extent of local racism into decision-making. The selection of cluster areas therefore needs to be both more systematic and more systematically researched, and also based upon a wider set of variables which are chosen because of their connection to successful integration. Employment, in particular, needs to be given a much higher priority in such decision-making since most authors agree that economic self-sufficiency is the key to successful integration (see Robinson, 1999).

Successful programmes have also tended to locate resettlement clusters near to pre-existing communities of co-ethnics. Settling refugees some distance from their fellow countrymen ignores the strong pull of such communities, with their cultural and religious institutions, their stock of housing owned by co-ethnics, their employment opportunities, and their access to the security and warmth of ethnic-specific social networks.

Equally, for some communities, access to co-religionists is vital to the success of a programme and its outcomes, and matching of refugees to settlement locations should be possible in a programme on the scale that is being proposed.

Finally, the evidence suggests that resettlement outcomes have been much better where refugees have been settled in areas where there is some local support for their presence, either from local people, local co-ethnics/co-religionists, or local people who share the same political beliefs.

The provision of support

The first lesson that can be learned from past programmes is that the most successful had either accidently or deliberately ensured positive media coverage. This proved vital in gaining public acceptance for reception and resettlement and is best achieved through pro-active media intervention at a national and local level (Audit Commission, 2000). Some of the consortia receiving dispersed asylum seekers are currently doing effective work in this field.

In the past, service and accommodation providers have been much more prepared to host and support refugees when it is clear that they will receive adequate, immediate and direct financial recompense for their efforts.

Resettlement programmes have fared better where reception staff, support groups, and all the external agencies connected with resettlement have been well-informed about who is arriving, when, and with what needs. This argues strongly for a joined-up information technology strategy that would allow all agencies to access a central database which contains all the information about a refugee that they might need and which is accurate and regularly updated. Different levels of security clearance could be written into access codes, allowing access to different parts of a person's file.

The more successful resettlement programmes have had an explicit commitment to medium- and long-term support that aims to facilitate both integration and community development. The Bosnian programme, with its Mid-Term Support Teams and its Community Development Workers, seems to be a model that could usefully be replicated.

Programmes where refugees have had some say over where they are resettled have been more successful than those which have been directive. Refugees asked to make informed choices are more empowered and enfranchised.

Finally, there is an argument for having a resettlement strand that links some refugees directly to educational opportunities. The WUS programme that resettled 1,000 Chileans directly into university towns where they had been offered places seems to have considerable merit. University towns by their very nature are cosmopolitan places with more tolerant populations, large stocks of rented accommodation, and ethnic minority communities on and off campus. Furthermore, most universities these days have established International Offices that are skilled at receiving and inducting overseas students, and facilities for upgrading the language skills of students who do not meet minimum Test of English as a Foreign Language (TOEFL) scores.

References

Adams, B.N. and Bristow, M. (1979) Ugandan Asian expulsion experiences: rumour and reality. *Journal of Asian and African Studies*, 14, 3, 191-203.

Audit Commission (2000) *Another Country: Implementing dispersal under the Immigration and Asylum Act 1999*. Audit Commission, London.

Bristow, M. (1976) Britain's response to the Ugandan Asian crisis: government myths versus political and resettlement realities. *New Community*, 5, 3, 265-79.

Browne, A. (1979) Latin American Refugees: British government policy and practice in Latin American Bureau (ed.) *Britain and Latin America: An annual review of British-Latin American relations*. Latin American Bureau, London.

Community Relations Council (1974) *One Year On. A report on the resettlement of refugees from Uganda in Britain*. CRC, London.

Community Relations Council (1976) *Refuge or Home? A policy statement on the resettlement of refugees*. CRC, London.

Compass Partnership (2000) *Evaluation of the Voluntary Agency contribution to the Kosovan Humanitarian Evacuation Programme*. Compass Partnership.

Dines, M. (1973) Ugandan Asians: one year later. *New Community*, 2, 4, 380-3.

Edholm, F., Roberts, H. and Sayer, J. (1983) *Vietnamese refugees in Britain*. CRE, London.

Evans, P. (1972) Survey cast doubt on the Town's case. *The Times*, 29 September.

Gibney, M. (1999) Kosovo and beyond: popular and unpopular refugees. *Forced Migration Review*, 5, 31-4.

Hale, S. (1993) The reception and resettlement of Vietnamese refugees in Britain in V. Robinson (ed.) *The International Refugee Crisis: British and Canadian Responses*. Macmillan, Basingstoke.

Home Affairs Select Committee (1985) *Refugees and Asylum, with special reference to the Vietnamese*. HMSO, London.

Joint Committee for Refugees from Vietnam (1982) *Final Report*. HMSO, London.

Joly, D. (1987) *Britain and its refugees: the case of the Chileans*. Unpublished paper presented at the Refugee Studies Programme, Oxford, 25 February.

Jones, P.R. (1982) *Vietnamese Refugees*. Home Office Research Paper 13, London.

Jones, P.R. (1983) Vietnamese refugees in the UK: the reception programme. *New Community*, 10, 3, 444-453.

Kay, D. (1987) *Chileans in Exile: Private Struggles, Public Lives*. Macmillan, Basingstoke.

Kohler, D. (1973) Public opinion and the Ugandan Asians. *New Community*, 2, 2, 194-7.

Kumar, S. (1973) Ugandan Asians one year later: Manchester report. *New Community*, 2, 4, 386-8.

Levin, M. (1981) *What welcome: reception and resettlement of refugees in Britain*. Acton Society Trust, London.

McCart, M. (1973) Ugandan Asians one year later: Wandsworth. Unsettled Ugandan refugees. *New Community*, 2, 4, 383-6.

Marett, V. (1989) *Immigrants Settling in the City*. Leicester University Press, London.

Marett, V. (1993) Resettlement of Ugandan Asians in Leicester. *Journal of Refugee Studies*, 6, 3, 248-59.

Patterson, S. (1977) The Poles: an exile community in Britain in J.L. Watson (ed.) *Between Two Cultures: migrants and minorities in Britain*. Blackwell, Oxford.

Robinson, V. (1985) The Vietnamese reception and resettlement programme in the UK. *Ethnic Groups*, 6, 305-30.

Robinson, V. (1986) *Transients, Settlers and Refugees: Asians in Britain*. Clarendon Press, Oxford.

Robinson, V. (1993a) Marching into the middle classes? The long term resettlement of East African Asians in the UK. *Journal of Refugee Studies*, 6, 3, 230-47.

Robinson, V. (1993b) British policy towards the settlement patterns of ethnic groups: an empirical evaluation of the Vietnamese programme in V. Robinson (ed.) *The International Refugee Crisis: British and Canadian Responses*, Macmillan, Basingstoke.

Robinson, V. (1993c) North and South: resettling Vietnamese refugees in Australia and the UK, in R. Black and V. Robinson (eds.) *Geography and Refugees*, Belhaven, London.

Robinson, V. (1995) The migration of East African Asians to the UK, in R. Cohen (ed.) *The Cambridge Survey of World Migration*, Cambridge University Press, Cambridge.

Robinson, V. (1999) Defining and measuring successful refugee integration, *Proceedings of ECRE International Conference on Integration of Refugees in Europe Antwerp Nov 1998*. European Council on Refugees and Exiles, Brussels, 118-125.

Robinson, V. and Coleman, C. (2000) Lessons Learned? A critical review of the UK government's programme to resettle Bosnian quota refugees, *International Migration Review*, 34, 1217-1244.

Robinson, V. and Hale, S. (1989) *The Geography of Vietnamese Secondary Migration in the UK*. Centre for Research in Ethnic Relations, Warwick.

Robinson, V. and Valeny, R. (2003) Ethnic minorities, employment, self-employment and social mobility in post-war Britain in S. Teles and T. Modood (eds.) *Race, Ethnicity and Public Policy in the US and UK*. Cambridge University Press.

Somerset, F. (1983) Vietnamese refugees in Britain: resettlement experiences *New Community*, 10, 3, 454-463.

Swinerton, E.N., Kuepper, W.G. and Lackey, G.L. (1975) *Ugandan Asians in Great Britain*. Croom Helm, London.

Sword, K., Davies, N. and Ciechanowski, J. (1989) *The Formation of the Polish Community in Great Britain, 1939-50*. University of London, London.

Tannahill, J.A. (1958) *European Volunteer Workers in Britain*. Manchester University Press, Manchester.

Zubrzycki, J. (1956) *Polish Immigrants in Britain*. Martinus Nijhoff, Hague.

2.

Sead Masic,
Representative of Bosnia Herzegovina Club
Ljiljan Northeast

Mr. Sead Masic was born in 1957 in Prijedor, north-west Bosnia. He completed Veterinary College in Sarajevo in 1981 and worked as a vet for 11 years. Sead came to the UK in November 1992 as an asylum seeker and found a job at the North of England Refugee Service, Gateshead in September 1993. In 1999 he was employed as Personal Adviser in West Gate Community College and then as Health Development Facilitator in Newcastle upon Tyne. In January 2002 he returned to the North of England Refugee Service as Policy and Development Co-ordinator.

Resettlement of Bosnian refugees in the UK

Introduction

This paper will discuss the resettlement of Bosnian refugees in the UK. I will cover the Bosnians in the north-east rather than in the whole of the UK, because I was involved from the beginning in helping these refugees to settle there, being myself a refugee as well. I will review two particular centres here, and the areas to which their residents were resettled. One is a reception centre in Cambridge, because most people actually from Cambridge were rehoused in Blythe, which is north of Newcastle. In comparison, I will review a reception centre in Newcastle, which was based in Gosforth, and the movement of residents there to local areas.

Background

Resettlement of ex-detainees from a number of concentration camps during the war in Bosnia started in October 1992. At the time, notorious camps in Omarska, Trnopolje, Batkovici, Manjaca and Dretelj were full of the Bosnians of all faiths, some of them being badly tortured and starved and thousands of them killed. You probably heard about some of the most notorious concentration camps. I was in one of them actually, there for about seventy days, just sort of waiting to be killed. It happened that the ITV crew came on 3 August 1992, and discovered one of them. They showed the pictures to all of the world, then within three days, believe it or not, the camp was closed and prisoners were actually transferred to other camps. Omarska, Trnopolje, Batkovici, Manjaca, Dretelj, these are all camps that people actually came from in the north-east of England.

Some people were transferred straight from the camps, others were actually released. They went back home and then from there they really wanted just to get out of their home towns and villages to escape the possible repercussion of people who had been looking after them in the camps. These people were walking freely around, and there was lots of revenge at the time. For example, from the camp that I got out of, a few people were killed even though they had been released.

So, it happened that a group from, for example, camp Manjaca, near Banja Luka, were fed straight from the camp to Karlovac, Croatia. Some of them were actually put to Sestine, Varazdin, and Gasinci as well, so all of these reception centres were actually probably established some time in the autumn of 1992. And most of the people resettled in the north-east actually came from these camps.

UNHCR and the International Committee of the Red Cross in negotiations with the Croatian Government managed to set up quite a number of refugee centres some of them close to the border with Bosnia and Herzegovina. People were provided with basic accommodation and offered the possibility to be resettled in some 22 countries worldwide.

Pre-departure

Ex-detainees were interviewed about their needs and to which country they would wish to be sent. One of them expressed clearly why he wanted to go to the UK: he wanted to be far away from the place where he was kept as a prisoner, but again close somehow, close enough that he can maybe, some time in the future, make a trip back to his home country. Most of them were thinking that they would be there for just a certain period of time, and as soon as the war would stop, they could go back home. Of course, this was not the case at the end of the day as you know.

The issue of information was badly organised. Most people did not know where they were going at all. There were just a few cases where people who had to decide where to request, found some leaflets about the country. Most of the people did not have any information about the countries which they were going to travel to and did not familiarise themselves with the changes they were going to face. They really did not have a clue about what sort of things they could expect in the countries they were going to.

Pre-departure waiting time was between two and six months. Many people were detached from their immediate families, which were still left in Bosnia and Herzegovina. All of them were extremely concerned about their safety. Some of them were reunited with members of their families at the centres but others left Croatia and were reunited later on.

Resettlement activities – an overview

In the UK there was a partnership. The Home Office was working with the Refugee Council, Refugee Action, the Scottish Refugee Council, and the Red Cross. They set up the Bosnia Project. All the people who came under the resettlement programme were entitled to very good service provision in reception centres all over the UK (Cambridge, Rugby, Batley, Kendal, Newcastle upon Tyne). Reception centres were well equipped and had dedicated members of staff who were covering the centres 24 hours a day.

People were warmly welcomed and they really appreciated it. It took them a long time to adjust to the British way of life, climate, food, but they felt secure and looked after.

The most important thing that the Bosnians found was that there was a possibility of family reunion. People who came with no families were worried as the war was spreading and it took a lot of time to be reunited with members of their families. They really appreciated the possibility that this could take place. They said that in the past, when they were on their own in the camps for two months or more (one of them was there for nine months) they were just so desperate to be near their families. So they were really satisfied as family reunion was given to them as an option.

Resettlement process – north-east

Blyth

Move from reception centre to permanent accommodation

Bosnians who were based at the Cambridge Reception Centre were offered a move to Blyth in Northumberland. Blyth was a small town, about 50,000 people. In summer 1993, people started to move to council and housing association houses. Most of the people were families with children. There were a few single people, who were later reunited with immediate family members. They got decent accommodation (houses and flats) and they were happy with it. Every now and then you could see a minibus coming, and support workers were trying to link them with all of the local service providers, such as education and schools for the children.

Initial support

But later on they found out that there was not necessarily the support available that they needed, especially in the beginning. Support workers and case workers were travelling to Blythe every now and then from the Cambridge centre to help these people cope, because there were not any services in place like the North of England Refugee Service (NERS). Support workers from Cambridge came to help with their tenancy agreements, social benefits, registration with GPs, and all other immediate needs. The Red Cross helped with providing free furniture.

By chance, I found out that I could volunteer for the Red Cross to work as an interpreter, so I went there to work with the first people who actually came to Blyth, helping them cope with a new environment, new housing, even new climate. (Since September 1993, I have been working at NERS.)

English language

People managed to find school places for the children, but the main barrier to resettling properly was language. English for speakers of other languages (ESOL) classes were organised at Ashington College. Tyneside TEC[1] gave the funding for classes.

This proved to be unsuccessful as there was not enough support to help people to deal with travelling arrangements. The classes were also rather hard to follow as the Bosnians were complete beginners and could not keep pace with the other students. They could not concentrate as well as the other students did either (because of problems back home etc). They explained this to the teachers, but it did not work and people lost interest and did not go any more.

Healthcare

Healthcare provision was actually very successful. All of the people were registered with GPs and were happy with the service. But they had quite a lot of dental health problems. I remember one lad had eleven teeth removed in one day.

There were some problems with interpreters though as it was hard to provide them in Blyth. Occasionally a bilingual support worker from NERS would accompany clients to appointments.

---

1   Training and Enterprise Council.

Employment and training

This is a very important issue for successful integration. Younger people who picked up the language more easily attended training in order to get better chances in employment but the quality of training determined that all of them left and continued to live on social benefits.

It was really in a very early stage. People were also preoccupied with thinking about what would happen to them in the future, because all of them had been given a particular status that they could not remain in the country with. They could just stay for a certain period of time and then go back home.

But then people really wanted to at least learn the language and maybe gain some other skills which could be useful if they went back to their own country. Yet there was no employment gained at all, simply because of the language barrier. I would say that among these people there were quite a few highly educated people. Some had their own businesses back home, others were very highly qualified craftsmen who wanted to do something with their lives because they felt very bored just being at home. They did not know what to do.

There were no activities really. NERS (which is based in Newcastle, twenty miles away from Blyth) found it was good to send outreach workers every now and then to help them with day-to-day needs. But NERS was overstretched because it only had five or six workers at a time and could not help them as much as we would have liked to.

Longer-term support and community development

There was no community development either. People did not try to organise themselves or get together to establish a group as there was not enough support.

They did not know anything about the British way of life. I would think that information would be really valuable if you are going to another country, just so you know what you could expect there.

Also there was nobody apart from NERS in Newcastle to help them to cope with their social needs and community development. They felt they were left on their own and did not get necessary support. I would say they felt 'betrayed'. Nobody wanted to stay in Blyth, there was nothing there. I remember a story that some Vietnamese refugees had been placed there. None of them are left. Some Chileans had been placed there. None of them are left.

As a result all of them (around 30 people) left Blyth and moved to other cities with greater population of Bosnians such as Birmingham, Dewsbury, London, Newcastle and so on. In November 1993, the reception centre opened in Newcastle and they found far better services. I will talk about these next.

Newcastle

Move from reception centre to permanent accommodation

The reception centre in Newcastle was actually based in Gosforth. People had security about accommodation, because we were working closely with the city council, and even some of the housing associations, in order to provide houses for people who were going to move out from the reception centre. There was actually a very good agreement made about housing, between Newcastle City Council and the reception centre, in order to find accommodation for Bosnians in Gosforth. Gosforth is one of the 'posh' areas in Newcastle, so people who were resettled there were really happy because there is no racial discrimination and racial harassment problems. People moved to houses and flats of reasonable quality and the majority wanted to stay there.

Initial support

The reception centre was again well organised and covered its clients 24 hours per day. In the reception centre, there was a team leader with support workers, interpreters, and wardens. It can be problematic getting people to an A&E department at 2 o'clock in the morning, so they were well covered and they had an interpreter at any time. Staff could always assist in an emergency.

It was crucially important to have adequate on-going support and dedicated staff. The people at the centre had their own support workers and a team leader who oversaw the project. Then at NERS there was a worker (myself) trying to rehouse people. We worked closely, and all of the staff working with the Bosnians were dedicated to this particular client group. People did appreciate that when they were going to call someone to help with some issues, they could be certain that they would get someone to help them.

Staff of the reception centre and NERS worked closely together in order not to duplicate services, but also to share experiences, support each other, and help clients with smooth resettlement. Every client was given enough time to access services as workers were dealing just with Bosnian refugees.

English language

Regarding their education needs, it was on-site provision (as I presumed people in Cambridge had). The people running the ESOL classes came to the reception centre and taught them.

I would also stress how important the work of volunteers was. People from the local community really wanted to help and they would come in and have face-to-face language classes. They were really happy about it. So children were going to local schools and adults were getting ESOL classes at the centre.

Healthcare

Health needs were also well covered in the reception centre, even better than for the people who had already been moved out to the community.

Employment and training

The process of integration was catalysed by the fact that some people were confident in their skills and found jobs, which was an additional reason to stay in the area.

Longer-term support and community development

Fundraising and social events were organised at the reception centre. In May 1994 people expressed a wish to establish a Bosnian and Herzegovinian Refugee Community Organisation, called Ljiljan.[2] The Community Development Co-ordinator of NERS helped to establish this Bosnian RCO, which was a great help in organising social and cultural events, mother tongue classes, activities for the children, and elderly and sports activities. The development worker helped us to identify the premises, to fundraise and really tried to integrate us into the local community.

Bosnia and Herzegovina Club "Ljiljan" north-east was very active, found premises, fundraised, organised activities, and made a positive impact on maintaining our culture and costumes, but also raised the profile of a successful and well appreciated RCO in the north-east which relied completely on volunteers. The Club has managed to involve various service providers, organise outreach sessions, and build a network of agencies working closely with refugees.

---

2   'Ljiljan' translates to 'Lily'.

Once people were about to move to different parts of the city, workers made sure that the move was organised as smoothly as possible. They also continued to support people for months afterwards. The Refugee Council seconded a mid-term support worker to NERS who continued to support the Bosnian community.

The majority of people remained in Newcastle. Only some moved down south. Bosnians felt supported enough to continue to integrate in the north-east. Once people from Blyth joined, the community was strong enough, becoming mainly independent and less reliant on outside agencies.

Positive experiences – media coverage and the local community

The work of the media is crucially important. At the time there was the war going on in Bosnia and every now and then you would see on television some images of the people suffering.

At the time media coverage helped with raising positive images of asylum seekers and refugees and particularly from Bosnia. Most of our neighbours were understanding, helpful, and kind to us. I would say that most of the people who moved from the reception centre to houses in Byker and Walker, in Newcastle, were well accepted. People from the local community went to their houses, they recognised that these people had suffered, and they offered their support. Some of the housing association residents went there every now and then as volunteers to help them cope with their needs, even if they had actually quite good coverage from the NERS workers.

There are Bosnian RCOs strengthening from day to day, and managing to get activities organised for children. People were actually really happy to get together and organise activities for the Newcastle Leisure Services Department, which worked well. A network of appropriate service providers resulted from a meeting we had at that particular period of time, with all the relevant ones – police, social workers, education, employment. We got together to find out how we could help these people later on.

Services – areas for improvement

Status

One of the main problems in resettling properly and in integrating into a wider community was a status issue. People were not sure how long they would be entitled to stay, what would happen once their "visa" expired and to where they would be returned. This impacted on their education and training so they did not study as hard as they might have or bother to retrain in order to find good jobs. They were living in an uncertain world waiting to be returned back home. The war was still going on and they just could not manage to sort their affairs at all. So they were always waiting, having their status extended year by year, and they did not really properly integrate at all. They were always waiting for something, with their bags ready to go back home and they just could not relax and say "well, I will now think about my future, I will get employment, I will change my career and I will really try to contribute to this society". That did not happen.

Education of local community

Local communities did not know much about the reasons why people were fleeing their own countries and some attempts were made to educate school children, students, and local residents. We did go to meet teachers at schools in order to prevent bullying (which did start to happen) and we organised some sessions for children in schools. It worked well because it was intervention in the early stages, and if you go to the children and explain about the presence of refugees or asylum seekers then this is the best way to do it from an early age. But this was not consistent.

English language classes

Language provision helped refugees to overcome communication barriers and NERS provided volunteers for one-to-one language tuition. This also made people use the language, rather than just to learn it.

Discrimation and racial harassment

Bosnians did experience some racial harassment but not that often and generally neighbours were supportive. Some families had to be moved from the houses in which they were living because of racial harassment. It took us two months though to persuade the local council that we had been harassed on racial grounds even if we are white.

Employment

Training and employment is very closely related to integration, but it was not addressed much and some people are still struggling after ten years to change their career and really get on with their lives. Some people attended training, changed their career, and managed to get jobs, but the majority of Bosnians are still struggling to gain confidence to apply for a job. Most of them are extremely keen and have mentioned that they will feel fully integrated once they start to pay taxes (meaning getting employment).

Mental health

Mental health was not addressed and the counselling sessions organised have not achieved a lot. Most of the people I have talked about are ex-detainees and of course members of their families have suffered as a result as well. Although all of the ex-detainees have suffered mental health problems in one or another way, our community has helped them by organising activities, social events, listening, and talking about their experiences. In a way this was counselling them.

A decade on...

Resettlement of the Bosnians living in the north-east was successful as available services were specific, focused, and long lasting. People have said, however, that you are in a process of integration from day one. That is not the case if you have not got your status sorted out. The employment rate is very low and people are struggling to find out how they would best fit into the society in which they are now living.

But over the years people became more confident, self sufficient, and independent. Establishment of the Bosnian RCO played a crucial role in easing the pressure of being marginalised, deprived (of cultural needs), and isolated. New generations became used to the British way of life far more easily than their parents, but families are still working hard to maintain our language, our customs and habits.

The most important thing is to try to raise the sense of belonging and contributing to the whole society. A Bosnian who is still unemployed said to me "the best contribution I can make to this society, and the day that I would say that I'm properly integrated is the day when I'm going to be able to pay tax. I'll really feel employed and contributing in this way".

We are well on the way to contribute and integrate fully into the host society.

3.

Ruben Ahlvin,
Senior Refugee Resettlment Quota
Co-ordinator, Swedish Migration Board

Erik Stenström,
Swedish Integration Board

Ruben Ahlvin is responsible for the Swedish Refugee Quota Programme at the Swedish Migration Board. His responsibilities include co-ordination and planning of the annual programme within Sweden, such as the final destinations of resettled refugees, as well as arranging the movements of refugees, and communicating with UNHCR and other resettlement countries in issues related to this area.

Erik Stenström is from the Swedish Integration Board. He is responsible for the integration arrangements for resettled refugees in Sweden. This work is also carried out in conjunction with local municipalities. He was also the chair of the Steering Group for the International Conference for the Reception and Integration of Resettled Refugees held in Norrkoping, Sweden in 2001.

Ruben Ahlvin: *suggestions for the UK programme*

Confirmation that the UK has established a quota for the transfer of refugees was very good news indeed for us in Sweden. Although we tried for many years to persuade the UNHCR to prioritise this work, the organisation lacked the necessary resources until several countries earmarked funds for the purpose at the end of the '90s. The UNHCR has responded by suggesting that the traditional resettlement countries should themselves take the initiative in recruiting new quota countries. We have had plans to integrate this work with other efforts undertaken within the quota framework, but are at present unable to carry them through. It is thus particularly heartening to be able to share the experiences we have accumulated now that the UK is starting a resettlement programme of its own. Not because our own process is necessarily the best in the world, but because we believe that with our more than fifty years of experience we can contribute some valuable input.

Allow me in all modesty to pass on a few key tips.

Try to keep the process under one and the same roof

There are surely just as many people involved in your process as there are in ours, and the fewer principals and senior players that can be involved the better. Figure 1 shows the partners in the Swedish refugee quota process. We start every year with parliament, where funds are allocated for the quota places. The government takes over and we, the Swedish Migration Board, are commissioned by the government to carry out the programme during the fiscal year. The Swedish fiscal year is the same as the calendar year. So January and February are concerned with the planning phase. There are some NGOs involved also in Sweden, but not so frequently as, for example, in the US, in Canada, or in Australia. But they are involved now and then, especially in the integration process.

Other resettling countries are of course involved, the Swedish Integration Board, the local municipalities, IOM for the transfer to Sweden. They are also involved if we want to carry out orientation programmes when the refugees are selected. We can run a short three or four week Swedish programme prior to the departure. Our embassies are of course involved, security police are involved in every single resettlement case to check out if they find any problems with those who are presented, but also if they have relatives in Sweden. Others involved include the UNHCR, the ICRC (the International Committee of the Red Cross), relatives, links in Sweden, refugees themselves. So as you can see, many, many partners are involved in the process, and I can understand that this is almost the same picture as you have here, when you are fully functioning.

Be clear in your relationship with UNHCR when deciding on the destination of the quota, the criteria, and plan for regular selection and transfer from the beginning of the year
This is so you have a balance from the preparations via the selections, the movements, and the arrivals.

Do not get stuck with decisions that will take a long time to alter if changed conditions in the outside world should demand it
Maintain a certain freedom of action. For instance, by retaining a number of emergency places that can serve as a buffer. Do not to be too strict when you assign your quota.

Carefully recruit staff who are to participate in selection measures
The head of the delegation in particular should have international experience and ability to identify possibilities rather than difficulties.

Draw on the experience of any traditional resettlement countries, to overcome any problems

Figure 1

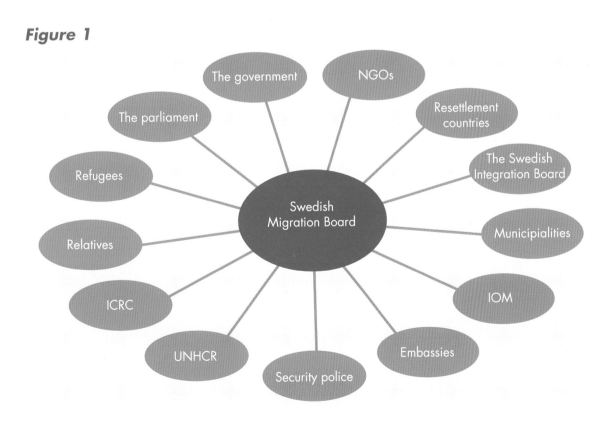

Erik Stenström: *Best practices and key lessons learned for integration of resettled refugees following the integration conference in Sweden*

The best practices and key lessons presented in this paper are the result of discussions that took place at the UNHCR integration conference in Sweden, in April 2001. The International Conference on Reception and Integration of Resettled Refugees (ICRIRR) launched the Integration Initiative, the exchange of experiences, information and views on the successful integration of resettled refugees in resettlement countries.

Two hundred and sixty participants, representatives of government organisations, inter-governmental organisations, non-governmental organisations and UNHCR, and former refugees, attended ICRIRR. Representatives came from 20 different countries: traditional and emerging resettlement countries and countries where resettlement had taken place on an *ad hoc* basis.

- *Traditional resettlement countries*: Norway, Finland, Denmark, Sweden, Netherlands, Switzerland, US, Can, Australia, and New Zealand.
- *Emerging resettlement countries*: Iceland, Ireland, Spain, Burkina Faso, Benin, Brazil, Chile, and Argentina.
- *Countries where resettlement has taken place on an ad hoc basis*: UK, Germany, and Israel (part of the US delegation).

As part of the preparations for the conference, experiences, knowledge, and views from Sweden were collected in the report *Bounds of Security: The Reception of Resettled Refugees in Sweden*.[3]

Universal principles of integration from ICRIRR

Although the policy and financial contexts of resettlement countries vary, there are some universal principles as the developmental phases every country goes through in both starting up and continuing a resettlement programme are similar. These principles should be valued as the result of lengthy and democratic discussions between 260 refugee, expert, and specialist participants in the field of resettlement from 20 countries in the ICRIRR.

"You can't feel grounded until you belong. You can't belong until you're accepted."

This was the overarching principle of integration that was agreed upon by participants at ICRIRR. Belonging and acceptance were considered the starting points for the two-way process of integration for refugees and their country of asylum, and for the individual empowerment of resettled refugees. With full acceptance and a sense of belonging refugees are better able to take such giant steps to rebuild their lives in a new place. The public, private, and community sectors have to work alongside refugees as facilitators to create an environment in which refugees can be empowered. From a refugee perspective integration requires a preparedness to adapt to the lifestyle of the host society, without having to lose one's own cultural identity. From the point of view of the host society, it requires a willingness for the communities to be welcoming and responsive to refugees and the needs of a diverse population.

The process of resettlement is fundamentally a personal journey through which refugees develop a sense of belonging, make friendships, and enjoy mutual respect in their new society. Participants considered a mosaic or a jungle was a fitting metaphor for an integrated society, where all individuals can feel appreciated and included.

---

3   Lineback, B. & Olson, M. (Eds) (2001), *Bounds of Security: The Reception of Resettled Refugees in Sweden*. National Integration Office, Sweden.

"Resettlement of refugees works"

This was another principle that participants at ICRIRR confirmed: the resettlement of refugees works, not only as a durable solution for refugees but for the host society as well. Refugees bring resources and skills to the countries in which they resettle and host societies are strengthened and enriched by the contributions of refugees. Most refugees integrate successfully into their host communities and most of the support and services provided by governments, refugee communities, non-governmental organisations, and the public make a difference.

Definitions of integration

Integration is a "two way street":

Integration is a dynamic, multi-faceted, and on-going process between the refugee and host society.

"From a refugee perspective, integration requires a preparedness to adapt to the lifestyle of the host society without having to lose one's own cultural identity. From the point of view of the host society, it requires a willingness for communities to be welcoming and responsive to refugees and for public institutions to meet the needs of a diverse population."[4]

Integration is "multi-dimensional":

"It relates both to the conditions for and actual participation in all aspects of the economic, social, cultural, civil, and political life of the country of resettlement as well as to refugees' own perceptions of, acceptance by and membership in the host society."[5]

The ECRE definition also highlights the time aspect. Integration is a lengthy process that starts upon arrival and ends when the refugee is a fully fledged member of the society.

Areas of integration

A glance at the agenda for the ICRIRR gives a good overview of the different needs of resettled refugees.

- the role of the media in preparing receiving communities
- building hospitable communities
- employment and education for refugee self-sufficiency
- refugee health and integration
- secure and affordable housing for refugee integration
- the needs of elderly refugees
- models for facilitating integration in the resettlement of unaccompanied minors
- special health needs affecting the integration of resettled refugees (for example, HIV)
- effective orientation as a critical component in the integration of resettled refugees
- information to refugees and to receiving communities
- placement strategies to enhance effective integration of resettled refugees
- cultural retention and adaptation in the reception and integration of refugees
- support networks in the reception and integration of resettled refugees
- language and communication issues relating to the integration of refugees
- refugee children and youth

---

4   Adapted from the European Council on Refugees and Exiles, *Policy on Integration*, 1999.
5   ECRE, *Policy on Integration*, 1999.

- survivors of torture and trauma among resettled refugees
- women at risk
- special challenges in the integration of refugees from countries with oral traditions

With particular regard to the role of information, the public should receive accurate and timely information about refugee situations. Receiving communities require additional specific information in preparing for the arrival of refugees in their communities. In both cases, the media have an important role to play.

Comparing spontaneously arriving refugees with resettled refugees

Sweden's experiences as a resettlement country go back to the end of World War II. Though the UK resettlement programme is just beginning, the UK already has a considerable experience in understanding and promoting integration and diversity/multicultural issues. In Sweden's experience, resettled refugees do not differ significantly from other refugees when it comes to basic needs such as accommodation, social benefits, English-tuition, training, and health issues. Resettled refugees are more likely to have spent time in a refugee camp, under particularly difficult conditions, and consequently may have greater health requirements in treating them for trauma. Also, unlike spontaneous asylum seekers, the government is able to plan for the arrival of resettled refugees. However, in general, refugees' country of origin, schooling, and other aspects may make a bigger difference to a refugee's needs rather than the process of resettlement itself.

Family reunification

Family reunification is crucial to refugee integration. Similarly, relatives and ethnic community networks can play key roles in successful refugee integration.

All countries seem to agree that integration is very difficult for the refugee if close family members are left behind in a camp: when refugees are asked what are the major barriers for integration, missing family members are mentioned first. Refugees may be completely preoccupied with thoughts of their siblings or parents, and send them money from the small allowances they are given. In terms of family reunification, the female family tree is as important as the male one.

Refugee involvement

Refugee participation and leadership are essential in the development, implementation, and evaluation of both refugees' own individual settlement and integration programmes. In a post-ICRIRR meeting in Oslo, Scandinavian countries complained about some less successful aspects of integration and asked North American representatives for advice. Deborah De Winter from the United States, who also was the facilitator for ICRIRR, said that the US took a big step forward in its resettlement programme when it realised three major principles for integration: 1. Refugee involvement, 2. Refugee involvement, and 3. Refugee involvement.

The responsibility of the public, private, and community sectors is to work alongside refugees as facilitators to create an environment in which people can be empowered. Enabling refugees to use their own resources and skills to help each other is a priority.

Material and fundamental needs must be addressed

Underlying the practical, tangible needs of refugees are more fundamental needs for dignity, security, social connectedness, and identity. Both these more fundamental needs and immediate material needs must be addressed. Responding to the range of needs specific to the refugee experience will improve resettlement programmes and enhance integration.

Partnerships and networks

Multi-faceted partnerships need to be continually developed and strengthened among governments, refugees, communities, non-governmental organisations, and volunteers.

Strengthening relationships between those working to identify refugees in need of resettlement, and the communities where they will be resettled, is important to the resettlement process.

Opportunities for resettled refugees to become citizens and to enjoy full and equal participation in society represent an over-arching commitment by governments to refugee integration.

Best practices in different countries

There are some developmental phases every resettlement country goes through. The early stages of a resettlement programme are a learning process for all concerned. However, even traditional countries of resettlement should continue to review the effectiveness of their programme and consider new approaches. Political situations in countries may change very rapidly, producing new groups of refugees with different cultures and needs who need resettlement, with which resettlement countries may not be familiar. ICRIRR gave participants the opportunity to discuss the problems their country has faced and how they resolved them, and discover and take comfort in the fact that different resettlement countries face similar challenges.

While it is difficult to compare the practices of different resettlement countries, there are good examples from which other countries can learn.

The US does have some very good examples on company micro-enterprise projects, for example 'easy way in' projects. They are successful in getting refugees into the workforce and also in developing careers. After six months, 80 per cent are self-sufficient. The US and Canada have an immigration policy where resettled refugees who are coming in a planned manner can be a perfect solution for filling employment gaps and for building prosperity. Resettlement is 'big business' in these countries where refugees are involved especially at a local level. A recommended web site is one in Toronto called www.settlement.org that provides help to refugees and NGO's on how to find a job and other aspects of integration.

In terms of a brief overview of some other countries, Sweden and the Scandinavian countries have a good reputation for providing healthcare. Refugees who have been traumatised, who are handicapped and those with special needs are well cared for. Scandinavia is also known to provide affordable and secure housing. Denmark also has a very sophisticated and efficient placement system. Norway's overall administration of the resettlement process is considered to be successful. Sweden specialises in caring for unaccompanied children and adolescents.

Illiteracy was also raised as an issue at ICRIRR, particularly when resettling refugees come from an oral tradition. Some good examples of how this could be handled came from Calgary, a project called *Pebbles in the Sand*, and from experiences with the Hmong population in the US.

Lessons from the ICRIRR for Sweden

Sweden learned more about the role that NGOs have the potential to play in integration. Until ICRIRR, Sweden had not considered that NGOs could be just as valuable as the local government in welcoming and integrating refugees into the community. Consequently, Sweden intends to re-evaluate the role of NGOs in its integration work.

Sweden has also taken special note of the importance of building ethnic networks. A careful balance must be maintained between encouraging integration into the host society and keeping one's own cultures and traditions. The fact that communities develop their own dynamics should be recognised. Sweden intends to review the practices in other countries to learn more about building ethnic support networks.

Sweden will also investigate further how micro-enterprise projects can contribute to Sweden's integration initiatives.

Reference

Lineback, B. & Olson, M. (Eds) (2001), *Bounds of Security: The Reception of Resettled Refugees in Sweden*. National Integration Office, Sweden.

4.
Joanne van Selm,
Senior Policy Analyst, Migration Policy Institute

Dr Joanne van Selm is Senior Policy Analyst at the Migration Policy Institute, Washington DC and Senior Researcher at the Institute for Migration and Ethnic Studies at the University of Amsterdam. She is also co-editor of the Journal of Refugee Studies. Her interest in resettlement stems originally from work on a comprehensive approach to refugee protection. Dr van Selm is currently carrying out research for the UK Home Office on a Review of Resettlement Programmes, and for the European Commission's Feasibility Study on Resettlement in the European Union.

Lessons on resettlement from the US and Canada

Resettlement is the organised departure and arrival of selected refugees, who cannot be locally integrated in a country of first asylum and cannot return to their home country, from a country of asylum to another (often developed) state which provides a durable solution to their protection needs.

In the February 2002 White Paper *Secure Borders, Safe Haven: Integration with Diversity in Modern Britain*, the Home Secretary announced the proposals for a UK resettlement programme. The programme would contribute to 'ways in which refugees, whose lives cannot be protected in the region of origin, can have their claim considered before they reach the UK, and are able to travel here in safety and receive protection.'[6] The programme will resettle 500 refugees per year, though the programme may develop once its processes have been well established.

With decades of experience in conducting resettlement, Canada and the US have very detailed and complex programmes. In this paper three key lessons of interest for consideration by the UK are described and analysed and some thoughts are offered on how they might apply to the British context. In doing this, it should be noted that 'lessons' from the policies of other countries do not provide a model that can simply be copied. Policymaking takes place in an evolving context, and the policies in both the US and Canada are in their own context and are changing all the time.

The three resettlement programme policies on which this paper will focus are:

1.   Involving non-state organisations other than UNHCR in selecting refugees for resettlement.
2.   The private sponsorship of refugees for resettlement.
3.   Loans for transportation to the country of resettlement.

All three of these policies are used, have been used, or are planned to be used in both the US and Canada.

This paper will first provide some background information on the US, Canada, and UK resettlement programmes. It will then describe the three issues outlined above for the US and Canadian programmes and the pros and cons of each policy approach will be considered. Finally, the paper will consider how each policy can be applied to the UK.

---

6   Home Office (2001) *Secure Borders, Safe Haven: Integration with Diversity in Modern Britain.* The Stationery Office, London. Presented to Parliament on 22 February 2002 p 52.

Background

Canada and the US are known as traditional countries of immigration. While the UK is not thought of as an immigration country, various new work permit schemes have meant that increasing numbers of people are arriving. Indeed, asylum seekers were, in 2001, less than one-third of the arrivals in the UK of non-EU nationals who intended to stay. In this context, the following sections review the current resettlement programmes of the US, Canada, and the UK.

US

The US resettlement programme has a ceiling of 70,000. This ceiling represents an upper limit and is not a target to be met or a quota to be filled. In fact, last year there were just 26,000 arrivals on the US Resettlement Programme (see Table 1). This was largely a result of 11 September 2001 and the new security concerns that followed.

The US currently operates three priority categories, reflecting the goals of its resettlement programme. These are:

P1   UNHCR referrals
P2   Specific nationalities who may be resettled, reflecting foreign policy concerns and the influence of domestic ethnic-based lobby groups
P3   Immediate family members of people already in the US from a small number of countries (currently the focus is on Africa)

On arrival, resettled refugees have refugee status, after one year they have permanent residence status, and after five years resettled refugees are eligible for citizenship in the United States.

Canada

Canada accepts refugees from anywhere in the world on its resettlement programme. Canada's overall target for resettlement in 2003 is 12,200 (see Table 1). It is a target that can be met or exceeded, or that might not be filled – although the latter would indicate a lack of success in locating and identifying refugees. The Canadian resettlement programme has three components (with a target for the number of refugees accepted under each scheme):

1.   The Government Assisted Programme, under which the federal government takes charge of, and pays for, the refugees after arrival.
2.   The Private Sponsorship Programme, where private organisations or groups take responsibility for refugees (explained in detail below).
3.   The Joint Assistance Sponsorships, under which the support for the refugees is mixed between the federal government and private sponsors.

A resettled refugee is considered a landed immigrant on arrival and therefore has permanent residence status.

UK

For many years, the UK has operated two types of resettlement programme: the Mandate Programme and the Ten or More Programme. Refugees under the Mandate Programme must have a strong connection to the UK, for example, either through a close relative who resides permanently in the UK or through having studied in the UK in the past. Candidates for this Programme are identified by UNHCR field offices and then referred to the British Red Cross. The Home Office's Immigration and Nationality Directorate (IND) carry out the actual selection and the vast majority of the people referred on this programme are currently accepted. The Mandate Programme currently resettles some 300 refugees each year.

Secondly, the Ten or More Programme resettles refugees with an urgent need for medical treatment that is available to them in the UK but not in their current country of asylum (usually a developing country in the region of their country of origin). The Ten or More Programme, as the name suggests, resettles ten or just a few more refugees each year, together with their immediate family members where this applies.

The government's proposals for the new resettlement programme indicate that the initial quota of refugees will be 500. This is expected to be in addition to the places under the Mandate programme.

Table 1   Facts and figures

Country	Asylum seekers (2001)	Immigration (2001)	Resettlement goals (2003)	Resettlement arrivals (2002)
US	61,700	849,807 persons granted legal permanent residence (so they may have arrived in previous years)	70,000 (ceiling)	26,000 (50,000 in 2000)
Canada	43,000	250,346 landed immigrants (ie people who arrived with permission to permanently reside in Canada, including resettled refugees)	7,700 government assisted 4,500 privately sponsored (targets)	12,000
UK	92,000	106,820 people granted settlement There were also 109,000 work permit holder arrivals (including 28,000 dependents); 339,000 students; 35,800 working holidays; 29,100 spouses and family members; 12,000 au pairs. The majority of these arrivals are not likely to settle permanently in the UK.	500 quota 10 Ten or more 300 Mandate (approximately)	420

Programme policies in the US and Canadian resettlement programmes

Involving non-state organisations in selection procedures

UNHCR referrals play different roles for different resettlement states. In essence, the UNHCR field staff review cases requiring a durable protection through resettlement and then refer the cases to a resettlement country. For European states, such as Sweden, the refugee referral form and dossier go through the Geneva headquarters of UNHCR to the state. For the US and Canada the process is somewhat different.

For the United States the UNHCR referral goes to an overseas processing entity (OPE), which will prepare the case for Immigration and Naturalization Service (INS) selection purposes. The OPE identifies which priority category, P1 or P2, the case comes under (for P3, a submission is made from the family member within the US. They file an affidavit of relationship at a voluntary agency).

Currently, only a few bodies operate as OPEs – including IOM (International Organization for Migration),[7] HIAS (Hebrew Immigration Aid Society),[8] CWS (Church World Service),[9] ICMC (International Catholic Migration Commission)[10], and IRC (International Rescue Committee). These bodies are paid on a *per capita* basis for those cases they prepare. There is no direct payment to UNHCR for referral, but the US does contribute earmarked funds (beyond its core contributions) for resettlement to UNHCR.

Once cases have been prepared, refugees are ready to be interviewed by the next INS 'circuit ride' in their region. INS personnel located in key US embassies around the world go on missions periodically to places where refugees are located for processing. The size of the programme means that often hundreds of refugees will be being resettled from a single refugee camp. This system is soon to be replaced by a new Refugee Corps. The Refugee Corps will be based in Washington DC, and teams will go out from there to determine which refugees should be resettled. The Refugee Corps will *only* carry out resettlement processing, where as the staff based in embassies are involved in many areas of immigration.

Canada, meanwhile, has processing hubs in key cities around the world. Visa post missions, which deal with both immigration and refugee resettlement, are present in the embassies in these cities. For general immigration purposes, the 'client' has always completed the majority of his documentation. For resettling refugees, the process is more resource intensive. For this reason, the new law (Immigration and Refugee Protection Act, 2001) establishes a procedure involving some assistance from UNHCR, in the first instance, in filling in forms. Essentially this is a new 'filter' between the applicant and the visa officer, called a Designated Referral Agent. Currently, only UNHCR is a designated referral agency, but there is a move towards having NGOs and IOM potentially play this role in the future. Up until June 2002, there was no need for a specific UNHCR (or other) referral, and there was no gatekeeper, because potential candidates for resettlement could simply approach an embassy or consulate. Since that date, however, a referral is needed, except in those locations where UNHCR is not present or has no role.

Currently under the new Canadian system, UNHCR identifies an applicant for referral to Canada and makes the individual or family referral on a standard UNHCR refugee referral form. If Canada is interested, it asks for its own immigration form (IMM 8) to be completed.[11] UNHCR can help the applicant in completing the IMM8 form which is then submitted to the Canadian visa post mission. The visa officer will then set an interview date and place. The interview will last for about an hour – including translation, decision-making time, and writing up. The visa officer will assess both eligibility and admissibility. The latter includes an assessment of the potential for self-sufficiency, although critics do point out that there is no standard formula or established criteria for what this 'potential' entails. In addition, potential security issues are identified. At the end of the interview a NO or a MAYBE decision is delivered. If it is MAYBE, then a medical exam, police clearance, and security clearance are carried out.

Finances are something of a sticking point currently in the Canadian shift. Referrals from UNHCR are considered to be part of the agency's core mandate and are not paid for separately by the Canadian government. The Canadian administration, like UNHCR officials, has considered a guidance/accountability role for UNHCR with NGOs doing the actual case preparation and referral work.

---

7   IOM carries out in-country case preparation in Russia, Vietnam and Cuba; case preparation for all the former Soviet Union in Moscow and also in Cairo, Damascus and Belgrade. It is to become the Balkans OPE.
8   HIAS carries out case preparation in Moscow and Vienna.
9   CWS carries out case preparation in Nairobi for East and Southern Africa and in Accra for West Africa.
10   ICMC has been carrying out case preparation in Croatia, together with IRC, but that is closing down at the end of 2002; in Turkey and in Pakistan.
11   IRPA seeks to simplify the forms needed for the process. An independently developed form that will provide the basic model for the new Canadian form is on file with MPI.

Pros and cons of involving non-state organisations in selection procedures

There are a number of advantages to the contracting of Overseas Processing Entities or Designated Referral Agencies. These include the fact that the government has an opportunity to involve civil society in the whole process of resettlement from its earliest stages. From the agencies' perspective this can mean that they have an active role from which to act as a safeguard on government decision-making, as their personnel will have a thorough knowledge of cases, and can raise objections if people they felt qualified were rejected, for example. Through having field-based staff, the NGOs will also have the opportunity to see the realities of the conditions from which the refugees are coming. This would also be true for UK IND staff if they conduct selection missions to select refugees. If NGO staff work on rotation in these posts in the field for a few months, they will be able to take this knowledge back with them to assist in the later process of service provision and assistance. This is certainly the case in both the US and Canada. In addition, staff members are sometimes seconded to UNHCR to assist in and learn about other parts of the pre-determination process.

Some countries outside North America raise questions about data protection if non-governmental actors become closely involved with the private and personal information of a refugee's detailed case history. However, this potential disadvantage to the case preparation intermediary model could be easily avoided with appropriate legal agreements between the government and NGOs and individual staff.

Questions have also been raised about fraud in preparing a resettlement case. There are concerns over whether coaching does in fact take place, and just how much assistance is given to refugees in planning their case interview, as well as in providing tailored information on paper. There is no research which shows that this has happened with staff who are nationals of the US or Canada and undertake this preparatory role for their NGOs. One way of dealing with this issue may be to give UNHCR some sort of oversight and responsibility role in the process. However, given that their role is to act as an intermediary between the refugee protection agency of the UN and the governmental decision-making authorities, this may cancel out the point of having a case preparation intermediary.

Summary of the pros and cons of involving non-state organisations in selection procedures

Pros	Cons
• involvement of civil society from the country of resettlement	• questions raised about data protection
• safeguard on government decision-making (through knowledge of cases)	• questions raised about fraud

---

Private sponsorship

Private sponsorship in Canada emerged out of a desire expressed by community-based groups to actively sponsor refugees outside of a government initiated programme. It was developed at the time of the Vietnamese boat people crisis, when community groups, many located in Ottawa, did not think the number of places (4,000) offered by the government to resettle refugees was large enough. The solution, put simply, was that if the Canadian public wanted to help more refugees, then they would need to help pay for them. The Private Sponsorship Programme is a little more than fifty per cent of the size of the Government Assisted Programme in 2002, and often exceeds the target set by the government.

Private Sponsorship involves the sponsorship of refugees by private organisations or groups of five individuals. Organisations, such as churches, and the student sponsoring body the World University Service – Canada (WUS-C), can make agreements (a memorandum of understanding) with the government at a national (federal), provincial or local level and thereby become Sponsorship Agreement Holders. The WUS–C, for example, has a national level agreement, as do many nationally-operated faith-based organisations, such as the Anglican Church. Many individual church groups use regional or local agreements. These agreements permit the organisations to bring a certain number of resettling refugees into Canada each year. Otherwise organisations may make individual applications, as can groups of five sponsors.

In ninety-eight per cent of cases currently, the private sponsor identifies the refugee in advance. The refugee might be the family member of someone already in Canada, and be sponsored by his/her local church group through the national church body. Or the refugee might be a student, who WUS-C selects in a refugee camp in Kenya or Thailand, for example.

Private sponsors agree to hold responsibility for the refugee's well-being for one year after arrival. This rarely goes wrong from the side of the sponsor, in part because the refugee is often a family member of someone already in Canada and known to the group sponsoring him or her. Also, by letting down his/her part of the agreement, the sponsor would not eligible to participate again. There may be more risk involved in the 'Group of 5' sponsorships, where any five individuals meeting income requirements can sponsor an individual refugee. For Groups of 5, the five individuals need to have income to a level that the government considers sufficient for both themselves and the refugee to live from for one year. Not all of the five sponsors have to financially contribute, but it is preferred that at least three of them do so. Church groups often collect money locally either through congregational fundraising or through the church's annual budget. Student groups carry out fundraising at different universities for the WUS-C, for example, by adding a small amount of money to the Student Union membership fee.

The sponsors are responsible for:
- refugee's rent
- bus pass
- furniture (often via a donation of furniture)
- deposits for housing and other necessities
- food
- incidental medication
- dental care (if not covered by the health plan for one year – or until the refugee can pay for him/herself if that comes sooner)

After one year, if the refugee does not have work, he/she enters the regular provincial welfare system. Often parishioners will donate their services (for example, the local doctor or dentist) to help out. Privately sponsored refugees can get access to classes, including English or French as a second language, on government-run programmes in schools, at YMCAs, and other such institutions.

With regard to sponsorship by faith-based organisations, officially no proselytising is allowed, however refugees often feel they must attend the services of the church sponsoring them out of gratitude, at least in the beginning.

Personal involvement and the existence of a network seem, to those with experience, to be important factors for the successful integration of the privately sponsored refugees in Canada. A Citizenship and Immigration

Canada (CIC) study[12] suggests that there is a difference in the employment levels of government and privately sponsored refugees after one year of landing. The study indicates that four out of five privately sponsored refugees are employed after one year in the country, while only one out of five government assisted refugees found employment. One reason for this may be that private sponsors may help individual refugees in their care to find a job (the income from which relieves the burden on the sponsor). Information from a paper by the RRM Policy Team indicates, based on a national database of immigrants to Canada, that refugees' earnings have, over time, been well below average during their first years in the country, but picked up after that.

The NGOs in Ottawa began a programme to give Government Assisted Refugees a friend or buddy a few years ago. This programme was intended to give the refugees without a private sponsor some of the benefits of the sponsorship programme in terms of close contact with Canadians, and someone to offer advice and assistance in establishing a new life in the country. The Federal Government adopted this model as the HOST programme and it is now implemented across the country. The HOSTs are intended to be friends of the refugees, in an equal two-way relationship, and not mentors, meaning that there is clearly some difference from the financial commitments and inherent tone of guidance and responsibility of the private sponsorship.

Private sponsorship promotes community involvement in the refugee programme. It provides resettled refugees with a strong support structure and permits Canada to offer a durable solution to many thousands more refugees than might otherwise be the case.

The US government attempted to develop a private sponsorship scheme in the 1980s, but it failed. The author's analysis of this is that the US sponsorship scheme was initiated by the government, and not by civil society. NGO groups perceived it as being a way in which the administration was trying to shift costs onto them.

Pros and cons of private sponsorship

The private sponsorship of refugees has some advantages that resemble those concerning the role of NGO case preparation entities. Private sponsorship gives the population and civil society a central role in the resettlement programme and in refugee protection. Private sponsorship is one way of ensuring, for example, that a proportion of the population of the resettlement country has close contact with refugees and hence may gain a greater understanding about what it means to be a refugee. This may help to counteract some of the negative images presented in the British media. In addition, private sponsors may be located across the UK and therefore dispersal of refugees may occur naturally.

Private sponsorship is a way to increase the number of people ultimately achieving protection through resettlement. Not only does it relieve some pressure on the financial aspects of the programme but it also allows the government to gauge how eager the population is to admit refugees in need of long-term protection by the level of private sponsorship requests. As private sponsorship in Canada focuses on pre-known refugees, it can also be suggested that such a system is likely to bring in family members of people who are already admitted that might not otherwise have been reunited. Immigration for family reunification requires a certain level of income for the refugee or immigrant in Canada, which a refugee might not be in a position to attain. With the resettlement programme, other sponsors can help to provide the money to allow family reunification to occur. The government's own quota or target can be used for those who have no family links.

---

12   Canada Employment and Immigration Commission (1981) *Longitudinal Survey of Indochinese Refugees of Labour Force Participation Rate and Unemployment Rate by Sponsorship Mode & Selected Characteristics.* Canada Employment and Immigration Commission, Immigration and Demographic Analysis Division, Ottawa.

Another positive aspect of sponsorship is that students and others with special characteristics and skills can be included in the programme. They may be more likely to have characteristics that indicate self-sustainability such as ability to speak English, a good education and so on, or they may have skills that they could contribute to areas of society where their skills are needed. The World University Service-Canada's students are one example of this. Some might argue, however, that this could contribute to a 'brain-drain' in the regions around the country of origin.

Disadvantages of private sponsorship could include mis-matches between sponsor and refugee, though this has rarely happened in Canada at least. Private sponsorship may lead to distinctions in treatment which are viewed as unfair or even discriminating, depending on the parameters on the private sponsors' scope to develop their own schemes and services. If upper and lower limits were in place, however, this problem could probably be avoided.

Perhaps the most significant complexity in private sponsorship is that the motive to begin sponsorship may need to come from the community. The government's organisation of the programme and its commitment to maintain the number of government assisted refugees would be one way of introducing a sponsorship programme and to relieve concerns that the government's motives are simply to shift the work and costs for the programme. However, the fact remains that the private groups and organisations need to invest in the process, be inspired by it, and be committed to act in this new role.

Summary of the pros and cons of private sponsorship

Pros	Cons
• involvement of the population and civil society	• requires community inspiration, activity, and investment
• potential to increase numbers	• mis-matches between sponsors and refugees (though rare in Canada)
• keeps resettlement for family members and resettlement for refugees with no links in largely separate programmes	• distinctions in treatment of refugees
• family reunification without the income thresholds	
• students and others with special characteristics can be included	

Travel loans

Both the US and Canada run a transport loan system. Transportation, the air flight costs, and movement onwards to the reception facilities is organised by IOM. Refugees are responsible for repaying the cost of their transportation (though sometimes privately sponsored refugees in Canada will have their travel paid for by their sponsor). The transportation loans in Canada are part of a revolving fund: the money that is paid back by refugees goes to fund the travel of incoming refugees.

In Canada, payments on transportation loans begin immediately, but for the first 24 months refugees have the option, if necessary, to lower the payments or defer. The government maintains a fund of CA$400,000 to pay the travel expenses/loans of the particularly needy (for example, those who fall sick or lose dependent support) after arrival. Many refugees do not realise that they can negotiate this deferral or reduction in payments, and some may oppose the idea of arriving in the country in debt. If the refugee remains in arrears, he or she cannot receive tax refunds (including the refund of the Child Benefit Tax), cannot bring in family members under the family reunification programme, nor are they able to get a travel document (including a Convention travel document).

CIC controls the loan collection. The Canadian government has a 92 per cent collection rate on the loans, which is important for maintaining public support of the resettlement programme. Smaller loans are generally paid back within three years. The government also has a team of 22 specially trained collection agents.

Payment for transportation to the US is initially made by IOM under its (discounted) Global Travel Programme, as is the case for Canada. The financing of the travel comes from the State Department and is replenished from the repayment of the travel loan. Voluntary agencies are responsible for collecting this loan, following the signature of a promissory note by the refugee, prior to departure. The collection of payments can be deferred until some time (months or years) after arrival. Twenty-five per cent of the loan is retained by the voluntary agency to cover costs. The loan is interest free.

While the loan system in the US has faced criticism, many staff in government, IOM and voluntary agencies point to it as a means of giving the refugee a 'credit history' – one of the most important facets of US life. This justification can easily be discounted as simply a handy twist on the part of the administration, but voluntary agencies with direct connections to refugees can give examples of where this has really been true, and to the advantage of the refugee. There is seemingly no serious penalty for non-payment other than the fact that the refugee's credit history may be damaged, impeding access to credit cards, loans, rental agreements, and other financial services.

Pros and cons of travel loans

Travel loans (or indeed other loans such as the loan for furniture purchases that Sweden operates) can make the refugees themselves feel like active partners in their resettlement. By having an independent financial stake in their resettlement, refugees may feel more empowered. What is more, with the travel loans in Canada and the US, the refugees feel not only like they are contributing to their own movement, but also to the future resettlement and protection of other refugees.

If refugees pay for a part of the resettlement process through a loan system, then the nationals of the receiving resettlement country may view refugees more positively. However, to be able to pay off a loan, refugees need to both be motivated about finding employment and must have full access to employment opportunities. They will not be able to pay off loans on welfare benefits. So, a loan system is linked to the provision of job-seeking assistance and might be said to be a stimulant towards finding work.

Over time, refugees are likely to seek access to credit cards, to mortgages and other normal aspects of life in the West, which often require some evidence of a credit history. A loan may provide the only proof of this ability in the first few years after resettlement.

However, the cost of travel may be high, for example, an individual travelling from Africa to Canada might be up to £2,000 even with the IOM travel programme discounted prices. For a family of six this is more likely to be £10,000 to £12,000. The burden of the debt can therefore be heavy, especially for a family where only one parent may have the (financial) possibility of working if childcare is an issue. If the individuals concerned do not realise they can restructure payments (or indeed if that facility is not made available to them) then they can get into serious problems, which might hamper integration and the establishment of life in the resettlement country.

Summary of the pros and cons of travel loans

Pros	Cons
• refugees feel active in their resettlement	• burden of debt
• contributes to future resettlement	• refugee can only pay back if employed
• nationals see refugees paying, not taking	
• develops credit history	

Translating the lessons for the UK

Involving non-state organisations in selection procedures

The fact that Canada has chosen, like the US, to move to a system in which some 'filter' entity is present in referrals and case preparation may be an indication that the UK should consider involving a case preparation entity in the selection procedure. The UK should contemplate which organisations are the right type of intermediary for the UK and how to finance the operation.

The UK may need to carefully consider what type of terminology it wishes to employ for such an intermediary. Non-state bodies are not actually part of the status determination or selection process in terms of actual decision-making, and the public should be very clear on this point. The real task of the 'filter' is to provide a step between the UNHCR referral, which is protection focused and the immigration selection by national authorities which may be primarily immigration and potentially integration-focussed.

Furthermore, it has the added function, if nationally-based NGOs are involved, of linking selection into the integration service providers in the country of resettlement, or if IOM is the intermediary of choice, of linking selection to the transportation process. In either case the NGO actor may also provide orientation services in the phase between selection and departure. As such, the term 'case preparation entity' may be a useful one. The organisation involved would prepare the documented case for selection and prepare the selected individual for arrival and longer-term integration.

Using such entities may not be necessary for a small programme in the order of just hundreds, as the UK is planning to start with. However, if the programme is intended to grow over the coming years, then it may be appropriate to build up experience and iron out any teething troubles by establishing an intermediary function for case preparation as early as possible.

Private sponsorship

Private sponsorship is generally supported by Canadian practitioners and academics who report very favourably on its impact and seem to view it as a form of 'best practice'. It must be stressed that private sponsorship in Canada emerged out of a desire expressed by community-based groups to actively sponsor refugees and not out of a government-initiated programme. As such, private sponsorship in the sense of fully financing refugees from the private sector may not be something a government can promote as policy independent of requests to do so from the potential sponsors.

However, the idea of private sponsorship can be related back to UK experience in the late 1950s when employers (generally coal mining companies) employed and housed Hungarian refugees arriving in the UK after a year or two in Austria or Yugoslavia following their flight from Hungary in 1956. The mines needed employees, people prepared to take on this dirty, dangerous and difficult work which was much needed to support the post-war economy. The economic situation has changed significantly, the nature of the jobs and the employers is such that they may not sponsor in quite the same way. The real question is whether the voluntary and faith-based sectors in the UK are motivated to play this important assistance role for refugees, and to instigate such a programme.

If formal sponsorship as such may not be possible in the short-term, Friendship Programmes of some sort might be, and could bring many of the benefits of sponsorship without the same input of private resources, as the Canadian government's adoption of such programmes has shown. The HOST and buddy programmes in Canada (and also in Finland) are also broadly evaluated as good practice by those involved in governmental and NGO-run resettlement activities. However, there is no quantitative or qualitative research to back up this sense of usefulness of these programmes. In Canada there is strong insistence on the programme being one of friendship and not of mentoring, and that does seem appropriate from the descriptions given. The UK's experience of the evacuees from Kosovo was one of public sympathy and many volunteers came forward for involvement in various ways. The Home Secretary in his October announcements on the resettlement programme (and other new immigration initiatives) referred to this public sentiment. This could be drawn on, with the appropriate information provision about the situations from which the refugees have come, to inspire more volunteerism and public involvement. It may be that working from volunteer assistance first (the opposite way round to the Canadian developments in sponsorship and friendship-assistance) could lead later to private sponsorship programme development in the UK.

Travel loans

Travel loans as operated by Canada and the US may not be appropriate to the UK programme. The Home Secretary has announced publicly that the resettlement programme is part of measures to counter the smuggling of immigrants. Consequently, it may be inappropriate for refugees to repay money to the government as a condition of the programme.

As mentioned above, Sweden also operates a loan, for the purchase of furniture. Unlike the travel loan, this loan is not mandatory. Some people may receive furniture through donation or may have a job well paid enough for refugees to purchase their own furniture. Similarly, the UK government could consider implementing an 'Establishment Loan' which people could use for a variety of self-selected purposes, all of which would be part of setting up their new life. It might be used for furniture, but also might be used for vocational training or conversion of qualifications, or as partial investment in setting up a small business, for example.

Conclusion

In conclusion, it can be said that all of the three policy issues highlighted in this paper have one message in common: investing in the resettlement programme and assisting refugees in integration will benefit them and their new society in the longer-term.

Careful planning is necessary to implement a resettlement programme successfully which, by definition, aims to give a durable solution to a refugee's protection need. Planning for and investment in such a programme should include all participants in the process: the government, NGOs, society, and the refugees themselves.

While the programmes from other countries cannot just be copied, they can provide ideas to be translated and implemented in the UK. Whilst there may be some teething problems, the resettlement programme will develop over time. Using others' experience to select and test ideas is a useful approach in building a multi-layered, multi-faceted, and useful resettlement programme.

5.

Gil Loescher, Senior Fellow for Migration, Forced Displacement and International Security, International Institute for Strategic Studies

Gil Loescher is Senior Fellow for Migration, Forced Displacement, and International Security at The International Institute for Strategic Studies (IISS). He is also a Research Associate at the Centre for International Studies and Queen Elizabeth House at Oxford University. He is the author of over a dozen books, including *The UNHCR and World Politics: A Perilous Path* (Oxford University Press). Before joining IISS, Dr Loescher was a Senior Researcher for the European Council for Refugees and Exiles in London and before that was a Professor of International Relations at the University of Notre Dame in the United States. He has chaired the external research advisory board for UNHCR's publication *The State of the World's Refugees*.

The need to address conditions in regions of refugee origin

As the United Kingdom embarks on a new refugee resettlement programme, it is important to consider the conditions of reception, the protection environment and quality of asylum, the processing of refugee claims, and resettlement opportunities in regions of refugee origin. To ignore what is happening in these regions is to risk future failure of resettlement policy and to place refugees and asylum seekers in greater danger.

In 2001 and 2002, as part of a team of researchers for the European Council on Refugees and Exiles and the US Committee for Refugees, I conducted field research in Kenya, Turkey, Syria, Jordan, and Lebanon in order to examine what is possible in these regions of refugee origin in terms of conditions of reception, protection environment, and quality of asylum, processing of refugee claims and resettlement opportunities.[13] While refugee status determination (RSD) is carried out in all these states, primarily by UNHCR, and resettlement to the West does take place, including by a selective number of European states, the conditions to carry out refugee processing and resettlement in these regions are barely permissible by international standards and are extremely undependable.

Reception capacity and refugee protection in East Africa and the Middle East

The regions visited for this study are extremely unstable regions where some of the major producers of refugee flows in the world are located. The bulk of the refugees in these regions – Somalis, Sudanese, Iraqis, and Iranians – come from countries where conflict, persecution, and other human rights abuses have persisted for years, making it unlikely that they will be able to return home anytime soon.

In East Africa and the Horn during the past decade, vicious intra-state conflicts in Somalia and Sudan have generated huge flows of refugees to neighbouring Kenya. Kenya also hosts refugees from the Great Lakes

---

13 See: ECRE and USCR (2003) *Responding to the asylum and access challenge: an agenda for comprehensive engagement in protracted refugee situations*. This paper draws upon the report.

and other parts of Africa. In addition, Kenya faces serious domestic instability as a result of inter-ethnic violence, particularly in its rural areas. There also exists a large Kenyan Somali population which Nairobi officials view as a potential security concern.

Conflict and instability in Iraq and Iran during the past decade have caused a spill-over of huge numbers of refugees into the eastern part of Turkey. Ankara's security preoccupation with its own Kurdish insurgency makes it particularly sensitive to refugee flows from Northern Iraq. Turkey is also a bridge between Africa, Asia, and Europe and therefore also hosts refugees from Afghanistan and Africa. Syria and Jordan border Iraq and have been major receivers of refugees from there during the past ten years. Syria also receives refugees from Iran, Somalia, Afghanistan, and Sudan and both Jordan and Syria have huge Palestinian refugee populations. Jordan and Lebanon are among the most densely refugee-populated countries in the world. At the time of writing, the short-term prospects for these regions are for new waves of refugees as a consequence of the global war against terrorism and the conflict against Iraq.

All these states lack the capacity to secure their long porous borders and coast lines. Not only refugees and illegal immigrants but also armed militias, arms, drugs, and other contraband flow freely across these borders. The numbers of illegal migrants, especially in Turkey and Syria, are much greater than the number of refugees; all the countries under study are major transit countries to the West. Hence, these countries are already overburdened with refugees and migrants and would be very reluctant to assume responsibility for more refugees, particularly at a time of escalating conflicts, human rights abuses, civil wars, and international armed intervention in the regions under study.

These countries have limited capacity and inadequate infrastructure either in their national economies or within their social and legal structures to absorb or to host refugees. Indeed, given the severe economic crises and environmental degradation facing many of these countries, it is questionable whether these governments can be expected to establish legal frameworks and institutions that would permit the absorption of hundreds of thousands of refugees and migrants living within their territories and provide them with essential goods and services and a range of civil, political, social, and economic rights not even available to their own citizens. Local integration for all but a few of the refugees in these countries is not a realistic possibility.

An important constraint in offering a secure asylum environment for refugees is the extremely limited roles of NGOs and civil society in these countries. NGOs operate in a very limited environment. Local NGOs have to register with government ministries and they are not permitted to function freely. In Turkey and Syria, local NGOs cannot directly access foreign funds for their assistance and protection programmes for refugees. Not only do Turkish authorities try to curtail refugee work by depriving NGOs of funds, but they also subject NGOs to harassment and intimidation. Human rights NGOs in particular are marginalized by both the government and the media and are depicted as subversive organisations threatening to national security and supportive of guerrilla and terrorist groups. A restrictive environment also exists for international NGOs. Hence, there are very few NGOs in Kenya, Turkey, and the Middle East and virtually no checks on governments or on the few international agencies that deal directly with refugees, such as UNHCR.

Refugee protection is increasingly subsumed under the imperatives of security and the strategic priorities of host states. Refugees are perceived as a potential or real threat to national and regional security. Since refugees flee unstable neighbouring countries, they often import with them the security problems of the regions they flee. Because host governments view refugees primarily as a security risk, they focus on adopting policies that aim to contain this threat, not on offering a secure protection environment for refugees.

Generally, both the governments and the citizens of these countries have negative views of refugees and associate them with problems of security, violence, and crime. These negative perceptions have begun to generate a backlash against refugees and Islamic groups across these regions, especially since September 2001. To deal with this security problem, governments such as Kenya have sanctioned policies that confine refuges to remote camps and that severely restrict their freedom of movement and right to work and that expose them to insecurity related to banditry, militia, and rebel groups.

The quality of asylum and lack of legal status for refugees

Most of the governments in the countries visited are not signatories to the 1951 Convention and do not have established asylum procedures. While Kenya has ratified the major refugee legal instruments, it does not have any domestic refugee legislation. Turkey has signed the 1951 Convention with a geographical limitation that excludes non-Europeans. Syria, Lebanon, and Jordan have not signed the international refugee instruments and do not want to be considered as countries of asylum for non-Palestinian refugees. They tolerate the presence of refugees on a temporary basis, but this tolerance is contingent on the understanding that UNHCR resettles all refugees it recognises.

None of these governments observe recognised international standards and refugees have little or no legal status and hence virtually no protection. Host governments seek to impose a wide range of restrictions on refugees and purposely avoid giving them any permanent residence status, insisting that they stay only temporarily. Often unable to obtain legal status, many refugees must contend with an array of threats.

The insecurity of their legal status can place refugees in dangerous and unstable situations, for example, when host governments engage in round-ups and relocations, or even deportation, sometimes to the countries where they risk persecution. The refugees we interviewed in these countries complained that poor security was their greatest concern. The human rights records of these countries are poor. Physical harassment, detention, and *refoulement* of refugees occur on a regular basis. Police and security forces arbitrarily harass, detain and arrest refugees. Corruption is rampant, especially among poorly paid border guards and police. Refugees and asylum seekers in most of these countries informed us that they consider themselves at risk of abduction, assassination, and disappearance by security agents of their home governments operating freely in host countries.

Kenya has no refugee law and refugees have no legal status there. While Kenyan authorities require most refugees to live in designated camps in the country's most remote western and eastern regions, tens of thousands of refugees, particularly Somalis, also live without assistance in urban areas, particularly in Nairobi. Kenyan authorities make no attempt to register refugees but routinely pick up refugees in police sweeps of urban neighborhoods and either transport them to the camps or deport them.

Turkey's legislation on refugees covers European refugees only. These comprise a minority of refugees in the country. Turkey does permit non-Europeans to register as asylum seekers and present their claims to UNHCR. To do so, however, they must register within 10 days with the Turkish police nearest to the border where they entered; the police conduct interviews to determine if they should be recognised officially as asylum seekers.

Access to the asylum procedure remains problematic. The 10-day filing deadline has led to the exclusion, and in some cases the *refoulement*, of substantial numbers of *bona fide* refugees. Moreover, the requirement that asylum seekers register with the Turkish police nearest the border where they entered, means that most Iraqis and Iranians must apply for asylum in the provincial cities of eastern and south-eastern Turkey, much of which remains insecure. Local police reportedly do not always register the claims of asylum seekers. They also regularly deport undocumented migrants, applying "safe third country" rules to northern Iraq, Iran, and Syria for asylum seekers who had spent more time in these countries than was required to transit them. Many of those deported may have had valid claims to refugee status.

Syria, Jordan, and Lebanon do not have refugee legislation and refugees live in a climate of insecurity. In all three countries, illegal border crossing, which is how the overwhelming majority of asylum seekers arrive in the countries, is a deportable offence. Lebanon regularly deports Iraqis *en masse* to Syria and other countries, thus violating the 1951 Convention which obliges states not to return refugees and asylum seekers – including those who enter illegally provided they show just cause for their illegal entry – to places where they risk persecution.

Syria likewise occasionally deports refugees, as in December 2001, when it *refouled* a group of several hundred Iraqis who had been deported to Syria by Lebanon without informing UNHCR or considering the protection concerns of the refugees and asylum seekers among them. In another potentially alarming development, Syria amended its admission and residence procedures for citizens of Arab countries. Whereas previously Syria allowed nationals of Arab countries (except Iraqis) to reside indefinitely in the country without applying for a residence permit, the new regulation requires Arab country nationals to apply for, and renew, a residence permit every three months. Citizens of Arab countries still may enter Syria without a visa. This change in residence procedures enables Syria to become more restrictive in its policy towards refugees if the situation changes there.

The Jordanian government limits to six months the time that refugees may legally remain in Jordan and does not renew identification documents after their first six months have elapsed. Although the government generally tolerates the presence of refugees after their documents lapse, refugees without valid identification are more vulnerable to a variety of protection problems, including harassment, arrest, and possible deportation. Iraqi government agents reportedly operate in Jordan and Jordanian authorities have reportedly *refouled* hundreds of Iraqi nationals residing illegally in Jordan.

In addition to threats to their physical safety and civil and political rights, refugees also face severe economic and social deprivations in their countries of first asylum, including lack of access to adequate food, water and basic services, health care, education, work, and housing.

Host governments seek to control or manage refugees by locating them in camps or restricting their residence to designated parts of the country. Camp conditions are frequently extremely bad. Kenya, for example, requires most refugees to live in designated camps in the country's remote regions close to the refugees' countries of origin. Dadaab, where most of the Somalis have been warehoused for over 10 years, is notorious for its violence. Refugee women, in particular, remain highly vulnerable.

In contrast to Kenya, practically all refugees in Turkey and Syria, Jordan, and Lebanon live outside camps. Assistance to refugees in these countries does not meet minimum international standards. Refugees' freedom of movement is severely restricted; they cannot integrate with local populations; they are refused permission to work; they live in limbo.

Lack of involvement by Western governments in the regions of origin

All the countries visited are plagued with protracted refugee situations where most refugees find themselves without freedom of movement, with few opportunities, and with almost no immediate prospect of finding a solution to their plight. As noted above, the nationalities that dominate UNHCR's caseloads in East Africa,

Turkey, and the Middle East – Somalis, Sudanese, Iraqis, and Iranians – come from countries where conflict, persecution and other human rights' abuses have persisted for years, making it unlikely that they will be able to return home anytime soon. It is also the case that there exist almost no local integration prospects in host countries in these regions. Until the international community is prepared to engage in a more comprehensive manner to tackle the fundamental causes of violence and inequality in regions of origin, resettlement really provides the only solution for the great majority of refugees.

Western governments have not given sufficient recognition to these protracted refugee situations and have not devoted sufficient resources, either financial or diplomatic, to these long-standing problems. There exists widespread donor fatigue with protracted refugee situations. For example, the situation of refugees in Kenya, Turkey, and the Middle East have been adversely affected by the cutbacks in donor funding to UNHCR during recent years. This means that some vital assistance programmes in Turkey have had to be stopped; it means that UNHCR has not been able to deploy the number of protection officers it needs at Dadaab.

Neither have Western governments fully examined the impact of international economic, trade, aid, development, environmental and defence aid and, policies on migration flows from these regions nor have they developed a comprehensive vision and plan to deal with migration and refugee problems. Despite the fact that EU governments at their Tampere Summit in 1999 emphasized the importance of EU partnership with countries of origin and transit and the establishment of a political dialogue and trade and aid links with these countries as guiding principles underlying a common asylum and migration policy, very little has been accomplished along these lines. The involvement of the European Community Humanitarian Office (ECHO) in the countries visited is limited exclusively to projects in countries of origin and non-refugee emergency projects in countries of first asylum. Even EU political engagement with countries of origin and countries of first asylum in these regions is limited to discussions and negotiations regarding readmission agreements.

The EU High Level Working Group on Asylum and Migration has so far failed to implement its action plans. There is a lack of close cooperation between the European Commission and ministerial departments at Member State level, a lack of sufficient resources and expertise, a lack of consultation and meaningful dialogue with countries of origin and asylum countries in the regions, and an overriding emphasis on deterrent and control measures rather than human rights, conflict prevention and capacity, building in the regions of origin. The HLWG Action Plan for Somalis, for example, includes only programmes for development or deterrent and restrictive measures for inside Somalia but target nothing for securing a better protection or asylum environment for the over one quarter of a million refugees in neighbouring Kenya.

To date, the role of Western governments in regions of origin have largely been limited to the adjudication of received resettlement applications. However, even in the best of circumstances, resettlement will provide only a partial solution to protracted refugee problems. If Western governments are to be serious about responding to protracted refugee problems in regions of origin, they can no longer neglect the crucial dimension of cooperation and dialogue with source countries and countries of transit and the need to become engaged in a more holistic and pro-active manner to regions of refugee origin.

Processing of refugee claims in the regions of origin

Apart from directly seeking asylum in third countries outside of regions of origin, overseas resettlement is practically the only means for refugees to access entry into Europe, North America and Australasia. While many Western resettlement countries have the mechanisms to accept asylum applications at their diplomatic posts in countries of origin or in third countries, few governments either systematically or frequently make use of these measures. Rather, most resettlement countries rely completely on UNHCR to make refugee status determinations and referrals to their resettlement programmes.

It is also important to note that none of the host countries under study have national mechanisms to process refugee claims and many of them are non-Convention countries. However, all of them tolerate the presence of refugees on a temporary basis. But this tolerance is contingent on the understanding that UNHCR will undertake interviews that will determine the refugee status of claimants and will subsequently resettle all of the refugees it recognises.

Refugees who manage to escape their own countries, therefore, have the choice of either travelling onwards, often illegally, to other countries to apply for asylum or to remain in host countries in the region of origin and apply to UNHCR for recognition and referral for resettlement abroad. Because UNHCR has effectively become the proxy decision-maker for Western governments in refugee status determination, it is important that the Office does not deprive applicants of the same set of fair procedures that they might receive if their cases were heard in Europe, North America, or Australasia.

UNHCR carries out RSD pursuant to the mandate given in its statute to provide international protection to refugees. Indeed, RSD forms a major part of UNHCR's work in the countries under study. In countries that generally do not recognise the legal status of refugees, RSD is the linchpin of refugee protection because it is often the only means by which those who need protection are identified.

Despite its importance, RSD is not given enough prominence either by UNHCR or by governments. This has been particularly the case during the past decade when the Office's activities and priorities became dominated by providing humanitarian relief in refugee emergencies and internal conflicts around the world. Individual refugee status determination is an expensive activity and donor governments have not provided UNHCR with sufficient resources to carry out this important function effectively.

In many of the countries in the regions of origin, RSD interviews and decision-making are carried out by local employees who frequently do not have the experience or appropriate legal training. The lack of resources has contributed to the increasingly frequent cases of serious corruption involving RSD by UNHCR in places like Kenya and Jordan.

The UNHCR also operates in extremely difficult refugee protection environments in the countries under study. There is a legal vacuum about human rights issues generally in East Africa, Turkey, and the Middle East, and there exists very little government or public awareness or recognition of human rights in these countries. The presence of UNHCR, like for most refugees in these countries, is tolerated by host governments. Hence, UNHCR operates many of its RSD programmes on a tenuous basis at best.

The RSD activities of UNHCR often provide the principal protection available to refugees in these countries and are usually the most important activities carried out by UNHCR in these regions. However, there is a pressing need to make the current RSD systems more accountable and transparent. These procedures frequently lack a number of basic legal safeguards.

Refugees in Turkey and Syria complain that UNHCR has not made publicly available its own guidelines or procedural rules for the conduct of RSD and therefore refugees do not know what to expect when they apply for refugee status determination by UNHCR. The standard of proof UNHCR uses to determine whether there is a well-founded fear of persecution is often unclear and most asylum applicants have little understanding of the criteria or process of UNHCR decision-making to grant or to deny refugee status.

In the countries under review, there are few, if any, legal or human rights organisations that inform and assist asylum seekers on RSD. Because most refugees are not provided with legal counselling or advice, many applicants complain that they cannot present their cases properly.

UNHCR does not allow asylum seekers to have access to their files, either to inspect them or to take notes or to have copies of material on file. While it is understandable that UNHCR files may contain information from confidential sources or agency reports that need to be protected, it is a basic principle of fairness that refugees should be permitted to know the information upon which their case is denied. Without this knowledge, it is impossible for applicants to challenge the information or reports upon which UNHCR decisions are reached. Nor does UNHCR generally give full written reasons when a refugee claim is rejected. Thus, most refugees are given neither adequate information nor sufficient legal advice to mount meaningful challenges to UNHCR decisions that are crucial to their future.

There exists no independent appeals mechanism for those applicants who are denied refugee status by UNHCR. Asylum seekers are permitted to appeal against negative decisions and to provide new information or to explain major contradictions or inconsistencies that might have led to the rejection of their claim. In all the countries under study, appeals are decided by staff of the UNHCR field office where the original decision was made. The majority of appellants are not re-interviewed and UNHCR decisions on appeals are taken on the basis of the applicant's file and any new information provided.

Resettlement opportunities from regions of origin

In all the countries under review, resettlement is an indispensable tool of international protection particularly because conditions for refugees remain so insecure in host countries. Since all the refugee populations under the study are protracted, they are all – in theory – eligible for resettlement under UNHCR criteria. However, globally, only roughly one per cent of the world's refugees are resettled every year, and there is a marked difference between the number of refugees who are eligible and who are in need of resettlement, and the number of available resettlement places.

In these regions, there exist a marked need for greater resettlement opportunities for refugees, many of whom have been stranded in these host countries for several years.

In Kenya there are approximately 255,000 refugees:
- at least 160,000 from Somalia
- about 65,000 from Sudan
- 20,000 from Ethiopia
- about 5,000 from Uganda
- some 3,000 to 4,000 from the Great Lakes region.

The majority of these refugees reside in camps and many of them have been in Kenya for a decade or more. There are also significant numbers of urban refugees, particularly Somalis.

Turkey hosts nearly 10,000 refugees and asylum seekers but this is only a small percentage of the approximate one million illegal immigrants in the country, many of whom have legitimate claims to asylum.

- The largest numbers of asylum seekers entering Turkey come from Iraq and Iran but there are also significant numbers of asylum seekers from sub-Saharan African countries who face substantial protection problems in Turkey and are under constant threat of deportation.

- Registered asylum seekers, however, probably represent only a fraction of the foreigners residing in Turkey who have a well-founded fear of persecution in their home countries.

Jordan, Lebanon and Syria host huge numbers of Palestinian refugees (1.5 million in Jordan; 370,000 in Lebanon; and 375,000 in Syria). In addition, these countries are also populated with large numbers of Iraqi and other non-Palestinian asylum seekers and refugees, many of whom may be in need of resettlement.

Jordan: About 180,000 Iraqis live in Jordan, many of whom are refugees. Over 1,000 Iraqis are registered with UNHCR and another 4,300 asylum seekers are awaiting a UNHCR refugee status determination.

Lebanon: There are some 4,000 non-Palestinian refugees registered with UNHCR. The majority are Sudanese and the second largest group are Iraqis.

Syria: Syria hosts over 3,200 UNHCR registered refugees, half of whom are Iraqis. In addition, over 20,000 Iraqis who are not registered with UNHCR and yet may be refugees live in the country. Long-staying Sudanese asylum-seekers are at particular risk in Syria.

In the past year and a half, the resettlement of refugees from these regions of origin have declined precipitously. There are several reasons for this. In Kenya, resettlement was halted initially because of a major corruption scandal involving UNHCR refugee status determination and resettlement referrals. The major resettlement countries, including the United States, suspended all resettlement processing out of Kenya pending the results of several investigations of the corruption scandal. However, the most important impediment to overseas resettlement which affected not only East Africa but also most other parts of the world, including Turkey and the Middle East, was the terrorist attacks in New York and Washington DC on 11 September, 2001. In particular, the suspension of refugee resettlement by the United States, and subsequent delays resulting from newly-enhanced security screening measures, have adversely affected the resettlement opportunities for tens of thousands of refugees in these regions. In early 2003, the United States again suspended all resettlement from the Middle East despite the fact that there were increasing numbers of Iraqis fleeing in fear of future conflict in their home country.

Because the US resettles more refugees annually than all the rest of the world combined, the UNHCR has particularly depended on the US for resettlement places in the regions that ECRE and USCR visited. In Kenya, during 2001, UNHCR assisted 904 refugees to resettle from Lebanon, the majority going to the United States. The United States accepted 499 of the total of 1,748 refugees resettled from Jordan during the year, and from Syria, the United States took 602 of the total 849 refugees resettled.

Although in Turkey UNHCR has maintained commitments from a relatively broad range of resettlement countries, the US still resettled the largest portion of UNHCR's caseload during the past two years, in 2001 taking 959 refugees out of a total of 2,747 refugees resettled. Nevertheless, in recent months there has been a slow-down in resettlement from Turkey affecting the prospects for several hundred refugees achieving durable solutions to their plight.

The lack of resettlement opportunities, coupled with the physical and economic insecurity that most asylum seekers experience in the regions ECRE and USCR visited, has led large numbers of vulnerable people to seek alternative means of gaining access to Western countries. Relatively large numbers of people, many in need of international protection and with valid asylum claims, choose not to avail themselves of the UNHCR's refugee determination procedures. Many fear making themselves known to the authorities out of concern of being detained pending refugee status determination and being treated like criminals by local police or security officials. Would-be asylum seekers know that generally only a fraction of all asylum applications are granted, that the determination procedures are lengthy lasting several months to several years in some countries, that they are unlikely to receive adequate social and economic assistance either from the host government or the UNHCR, and that they may have a better chance of getting to the West if they remain outside the official system and utilize the services of trafficker and smuggling organisations.

6.

James Milner,
Student Associate, Refugee Studies Centre,
University of Oxford

James Milner is a doctoral student at the Refugee Studies Centre, University of Oxford, writing on host-state security, burden sharing, and refugee protection in Africa. In 2000–2001, he was a Resettlement Consultant for UNHCR in Cameroon and Guinea. In 2002, he was a Consultant for the Resettlement Section, Department of International Protection, UNHCR Headquarters, where he was responsible for revising and expanding the procedural and management chapters of the UNHCR Resettlement Handbook.[14]

Recent developments in international resettlement policy: implications for the UK programme

Introduction

The focus of this paper is international resettlement policy. This policy has developed since 1995 through various tripartite forums, involving resettlement countries, non-governmental organisations (NGOs), and the Office of the United Nations High Commissioner for Refugees (UNHCR). It has been most clearly articulated during the recent Global Consultations on International Protection[15] and figures prominently in the Agenda for Protection[16] and in the 2001 Conclusion on International Protection of the Executive Committee of the High Commissioner's Programme (EXCOM).[17]

These discussions and conclusions have consistently highlighted the three functions of resettlement: as a tool of international protection; as a durable solution; and, as an expression of international solidarity with countries of first asylum. The goal of this paper is to outline the elements of this developing body of policy centred on these three functions, and to argue that these policies could effectively inform the future direction of the UK resettlement programme.

The paper begins by providing a brief historical overview of international resettlement efforts from the end of World War II. Focusing on the successes and failures of the Comprehensive Plan of Action (CPA) for Indochinese refugees, the paper will outline structural changes in the organisation and co-ordination of international resettlement efforts in the mid-1990s, which provided the forum for the development of international resettlement policy.

---

14   The argument of this paper is based on the author's experience as a Resettlement Consultant with the UNHCR and drawn from research conducted as part of a trans-Atlantic research project between the European Council on Refugees and Exiles (ECRE) and the US Committee for Refugees, funded by the German Marshall Fund, on the feasibility of joint EU resettlement and asylum processing in the regions of origin. See: ECRE and USCR, *Responding to the Asylum and Access Challenge: an agenda for comprehensive engagement in protracted refugee situations*, April 2003.

15   See: UNHCR, Executive Committee of the High Commissioner's Programme (EXCOM), *Global Consultations on International Protection: Report of the Fourth Meeting in the Third Track (22 – 24 May 2002)*, Standing Committee, 24th Meeting, EC/GC/02/10, 14 June 2002; UNHCR, *Strengthening and Expanding Resettlement Today: Dilemmas, Challenges and Opportunities*, Global Consultations on International Protection, Third Track, Fourth Meeting, EC/GC/02/7, 25 April 2002; UNHCR, *Nordic Regional Meeting 'Resettlement as a Multi-Faceted Protection Tool and its Relationship to Migration'*, Oslo (6–7 November 2001), Global Consultations on International Protection, 4th Regional Meeting.

16   UNHCR, EXCOM, *Agenda for Protection*, Standing Committee, 24th Meeting, EC/52/SC/CRP.9, 11 June 2002.

17   UNHCR, EXCOM, Conclusion on International Protection. No. 90 (LII), 2001.

The paper will then turn to the three functions of resettlement, and lessons for the UK resettlement programme. Special attention will be paid to the international solidarity and burden-sharing function of resettlement. Here, the importance of working within the tripartite resettlement structure will be identified as the most effective way of maximising the protection benefits of the UK's limited resettlement quota. Given the intended reliance of the UK programme on UNHCR to identify and refer resettlement cases, the paper will also outline constraints currently limiting UNHCR's resettlement activities in the field. It will be argued that if the UK is to rely on UNHCR to play a crucial identification role in its resettlement programme, then serious attention must be paid to the constraints currently faced by the organisation.

Finally, the paper will turn to a consideration of what resettlement is not, and examine the relationship between resettlement and asylum programmes. Drawing on UNHCR briefing papers, this paper will argue that resettlement is not a migration management tool and that resettlement is a compliment to asylum, not a substitute.

Overview of early international resettlement efforts

To understand the significance and focus of recent international resettlement policy, it is important to remember that resettlement played a prominent role in the international response to refugee movements from the end of World War II through to the implementation of the Comprehensive Plan of Action (CPA) for Indochinese refugees. The course and development of these programmes laid an important foundation for future resettlement discussions.

Resettlement has been a feature of the international response to a number of refugee crises since the emergence of the international refugee regime. In 1947, the International Refugee Organisation (IRO) was founded to find solutions for those refugees remaining in Europe after World War II. Motivated by the objective of ensuring peace and stability in Europe in the aftermath of the war, and concerned with the prospects of returning displaced persons to Communist regimes, overseas resettlement was identified by the Western powers as the preferable solution. During the next four years, the IRO facilitated the resettlement of over a million people, primarily to countries outside Europe, while repatriating only 73,000.[18]

Resettlement evolved and expanded considerably in the context of the Cold War. Western governments, led by the United States, used resettlement not only as a tool of protection for those in need, but also as a means of highlighting the failures of Communist regimes.[19] In this way, motivations to engage in large-scale resettlement tended to be focused on particular groups of people and were motivated by the foreign policy of Western states.[20]

Such considerations were particularly evident in the Western response to the estimated 200,000 refugees who fled to Austria and Yugoslavia following the Soviet invasion of Hungary in 1956. As later reported by UNHCR, "there was a feeling of revulsion throughout the Western world at the turn of events in Hungary and considerable guilt that more had not been done to assist the Hungarian people in their struggle for democracy."[21] By the end of 1958, over 15 countries had offered resettlement places to Hungarian refugees. Nearly 200,000 Hungarian refugees were eventually resettled in third countries at a global cost of $100 million.

---

18   See: Gil Loescher, *The UNHCR and World Politics: A Perilous Path*, Oxford: Oxford University Press, 2001, 39–43.
19   This 'exile-oriented' solution to refugee problems came to dominate both government and UNHCR responses during the Cold War. See: Gervase Coles, *Approaches to the refugee problem today* in Gil Loescher and Liala Monahan (eds.), Refugees in International Relations, Oxford: Oxford University Press, 1989.
20   See: Gil Loescher and John Scanlan, *Calculated Kindness: Refugees and America's Half-open Door*, New York: The Free Press, 1986.
21   UNHCR, *State of the Word's Refugees: Fifty years of humanitarian service*, Oxford: Oxford University Press, 2000, 32.

The generous and rapid response of the international community to the Hungarian exodus stood in marked contrast to the attitude of governments towards the residual caseload of tens of thousands of displaced people within Europe after World War II still in need of a solution towards the end of the 1950s. In response to this protracted refugee situation, British refugee advocates, backed by NGOs and UNHCR, called for international action.[22] This pressure resulted in 1959 being declared 'World Refugee Year' by the United Nations, and the initiation of a comprehensive response to those remaining both in camps and outside of camps. UNHCR appealed to resettlement governments to provide both funds and resettlement quotas, following this the protracted refugee problem was finally resolved by the mid-1960s.[23]

By the early 1970s, the international community's increasing focus on human rights led to a motivation to "rescue" the "innocent victims" of repressive regimes beyond the front-lines of the Cold War. These sentiments underlay the motivations for resettling over 40,000 Ugandan Asians facing expulsion by Idi Amin in 1972 and of over 5,000 Latin American refugees following threats of *refoulement* by the military regime in Chile in September 1973. While the total number of refugees resettled from Uganda and Chile are not on the same scale as the response to Hungary, the way in which the refugees were processed for resettlement, especially in Uganda, created an important precedent. UNHCR, the International Organization for Migration (IOM) and the International Committee of the Red Cross (ICRC) cooperated to establish "safe-havens" inside Uganda for the sheltering of those under expulsion and pending their resettlement.

By far the "largest and most dramatic example of resettlement in modern times"[24] involved the international response to the Indo-Chinese refugee crisis in south-east Asia. The consolidation of communist south-east Asian regimes in 1975 resulted in an estimated three million people fleeing Vietnam, Cambodia, and Laos in the following two decades. Most fled in small boats, and many died in shipwrecks or were targeted by pirates. Humanitarianism, coupled with the geopolitical interests of the United States, motivated Western states to recognise the 'boat people' as refugees *prima facie* and to resettle them. More than 550,000 Indo-Chinese sought asylum in south-east Asia between 1975 and 1979, of which 200,000 were resettled.[25]

As arrivals continued to exceed resettlement quotas, regional states declared in June 1979 that they had "reached the limit of their endurance and decided that they would not accept new arrivals."[26] This reluctance, and reports of regional states pushing boats carrying asylum seekers away from their shores, led to an International Conference on Indo-Chinese Refugees in July 1979. States agreed that worldwide resettlement quotas would be doubled, that the boat people would be recognised as refugees *prima facie*, that illegal departures would be prevented, and that regional processing centres would be established. The result was a formalized *quid pro quo*: resettlement to Western states in exchange for assurances of first asylum in the region.

The immediate results were positive: resettlement increased, 'push-backs' ended and arrival rates fell dramatically as heavy penalties were imposed on clandestine departures. By 1988, however, the number of asylum seekers began to rise dramatically as promises of resettlement resulted in a dramatic pull factor. Believing that these new arrivals no longer warranted automatic refugee status, Western countries introduced selective criteria and reduced resettlement quotas. In response, regional asylum countries returned to earlier policies of preventing arrivals, including push-backs.

22   Yéfime Zarjevski, *A Future Preserved: International Assistance to Refugees*, Oxford: Pergamon Press for the Office of the United Nations High Commissioner for Refugees, 1988, p. 88–90.
23   This response to the residual groups "left behind after successive selection missions have picked those people who were young and healthy and met rigid resettlement criteria" (UN High Commissioner for Refugee, 28 October 1958), motivated by humanitarian concern, illustrates the potential of a comprehensive resettlement effort to address the needs of protracted and neglected refugee caseloads. This program is an often-forgotten precedent for addressing the durable solution and protection needs of refugees for whom neither local integration nor repatriation are viable options.
24   UNHCR Resettlement Handbook (July 1997), I/5.
25   UNHCR, *State of the Word's Refugees*, 2000, 84.
26   *Ibid*, 83.

In light of this new reality, the Second International Conference on Indo-Chinese refugees was convened in June 1989 and concluded by adopting the CPA. The CPA contained five mechanisms through which the countries of origin, countries of first asylum, and resettlement countries cooperated to resolve the refugee crisis in south-east Asia: an Orderly Departure Program (ODP) to prevent clandestine departures, guaranteed temporary asylum by countries in the region, individual refugee status determination for all new arrivals, resettlement to third countries for those recognised as refugees, and facilitated return for rejected claimants.[27] As such, resettlement was used as part of a comprehensive response to a complex refugee situation.

Notwithstanding a number of criticisms,[28] the CPA is seen to have generally achieved its objectives of reducing the number of clandestine departures, managing the flow of migrants from Indo-China and of finding extra-regional durable solutions for recognised refugees. In 1989, roughly 70,000 Vietnamese sought asylum in south-east Asia. By 1992, this number had fallen to 41.[29] At the same time, over 1,950,000 refugees had been resettled by the end of the CPA in 1995; 1,250,000 to the United States alone. On this basis, the CPA is seen by many as a success, and a dramatic example of the possibilities of burden sharing arrangements to address refugee crises.

Recent developments in resettlement policy and practice

While the CPA was arguably the greatest example of resettlement, it was also a source of its undoing. As part of a comprehensive review of its global resettlement activities, UNHCR noted in 1994 that "the disenchantment with resettlement" which followed the Indo-Chinese experience "has had a negative effect on UNHCR's capacity to effectively perform resettlement functions."[30] This 'disenchantment with resettlement', on the part of traditional resettlement countries and UNHCR, resulted in the reduction in resettlement quotas and a renewed emphasis on return and reintegration as the preferred durable solution.[31]

This characterization of the 'end of the era of resettlement' proved, however, to be an exaggeration. Significant developments have occurred in the area of resettlement since UNHCR's 1995 Evaluation Report on Resettlement Activities. Highlighting the "need to improve the dialogue and cooperation between UNHCR and all partners involved in resettlement", including resettlement countries, NGOs and IOM, the report called upon UNHCR to "establish formal mechanisms of systematic consultation with partners". In June 1995, a Working Group on Resettlement was established, involving ten traditional resettlement countries[32] and with discussion focusing on annual resettlement quotas. At roughly the same time, consultations with NGOs were organised in North America and Europe to ensure that valuable NGO contributions to the resettlement process would be maintained.

---

27   See: UNHCR, *International Conference on Indo-Chinese Refugees. Report of the Secretary General [Annex: Declaration and Comprehensive Plan of Action (CPA)]*, http://www.unhcr.ch (cited 1 March 2002).
28   The CPA has been criticized for a number of reasons. First, RSD procedures in the region varied considerably, were often inadequate and were premised on the assumption that the 'boat people' were predominantly economic migrants, not refugees. Second, the low standards of care and maintenance in asylum centres were reported to frequently violate international standards, motivated by a desire to deter future asylum seekers. Third, scholars have argued that the conditionality of asylum for resettlement runs contrary to the principles of international law. Fourth, incidences of forced return of failed asylum seekers were frequently denounced by human rights organisations. Finally, it has been argued that the CPA created a 'market system' where immigration and political considerations overshadowed asylum considerations and which was dominated by US geopolitical interests. See: Shamsul Bari, Refugee Status Determination under the Comprehensive Plan of Action (CPA): A Personal Assessment, *International Journal of Refugee Law*, Vol. 4, no. 4, 1992; W. Courtland Robinson, *Terms of Refuge: The Indochinese Exodus and the International Response*, London: Zed Books, 1998; Astri Shurke, Burden Sharing during Refugee Emergencies: The Logic of Collective versus National Action, *Journal of Refugee Studies*, Vol. 11, no. 4, 1998.
29   UNHCR, *State of the World's refugees*, 2000, 84.
30   UNHCR, *Resettlement in the 1990s: A Review of Policy and Practice*, October 1994, 1.
31   See: B.S. Chimni, *From resettlement to involuntary repatriation: towards a critical history of durable solutions to refugee problems*, New Issues in Refugee Research, Working Paper No. 2, UNHCR, May 1999.
32   US, Canada, Australia, New Zealand, Finland, Sweden, Norway, Denmark, Switzerland and the Netherlands.

These two tracks were brought together in Geneva in October 1995 during the first formal Consultations with Governments and NGOs. These Consultations have subsequently been convened on an annual basis, and have come to be known as the Annual Tripartite Consultations on Resettlement (ATC). This annual event has proven to be a valuable forum for enhancing partnerships, developing joint strategies for addressing resettlement needs, information sharing, and the development of a more harmonised approach to resettlement.

It was through this process of consultation that UNHCR was able to develop and issue the *Resettlement Handbook* in July 1997, now used by all UNHCR field offices in the process of identifying and processing refugees in need of resettlement. Through on-going consultation and the development of partnerships, resettlement has developed into a global tool of international protection in recent years as the number of resettlement countries and resettled nationalities have continued to increase.[33] A total of 17 countries now cooperate with UNHCR's resettlement efforts by making available an annual resettlement quota of almost 100,000 refugees a year from all regions of the world.[34]

The functions of resettlement

The Tripartite process has also facilitated the progressive development of resettlement policy in recent years, focusing on the function of resettlement:

1. as a tool of international protection for individual refugees;
2. as a durable solution for protracted refugee situations; and
3. as an expression of international solidarity with countries of first asylum.

These three functions have been central to recent discussions of international resettlement efforts, especially through the Global Consultations on International Protection and the resulting Agenda for Protection. These functions have been endorsed by a wide range of governments, both resettlement countries and non-resettlement countries. While not binding on the UK, allowing these three functions to guide the development of the UK resettlement programme would help ensure that the programme is in-line with international standards, benefits from the lessons of other resettlement countries, and maximises the protection benefits of a limited resettlement quota by cooperating in global resettlement efforts.

Resettlement is a tool of international protection for individual refugees

Resettlement is, first and foremost, a tool for meeting the special needs of refugees whose life, liberty, safety, health or other fundamental human rights are at risk in the country where they sought refuge.[35] It is generally recognised by all resettlement countries that protection is, and should be, at the core of any resettlement programme, and that resettlement decisions should be motivated by the protection needs of refugees.

There are both qualitative and quantitative challenges relating to the protection function of resettlement. Not only is there a challenge to ensure that there are sufficient resettlement opportunities available for those refugees requiring resettlement as a means of protection, but systems and procedures need to be responsive, especially to urgent and special protection needs. To this end, UNHCR has argued that "the integrity of the

---

33   See: *Internationalizing Resettlement* in *Opening Remarks by the Assistant High Commissioner for Refugees, Mr. Soren Jessen-Petersen*, Annual Tripartite Consultations on Resettlement, Geneva, 20 June 2001.

34   In 2001, those countries (with their quotas) were: Australia (4,000), Benin (240 over 2 years), Brazil (30), Burkina Faso (100), Canada (7,300), Chile (65), Denmark (517), Finland (750), Iceland (23), Ireland (10 cases), the Netherlands (500), Norway (1,500), New Zealand (750), Spain (no specific quota), Sweden (1,375), Switzerland (no specific quota), US (80,000).

35   UNHCR Resettlement Handbook (July 1997), I/1.

[resettlement] process depends upon how the cases are profiled and how rapidly they can be accepted. The system has to be capable of responding both to special needs and to the urgency of the required response".[36]

In the context of the proposed workings of the UK resettlement programme,[37] two important questions must be asked to ensure that this protection function can be effectively realised. Firstly, how can this protection be extended quickly, and secondly, how should the status of individuals be balanced against their need for resettlement?[38]

The first question relates to ensuring that a resettlement programme is responsive to more urgent protection needs. According to UNHCR's procedures, there are three prioritisations for resettlement: Emergency – where a refugee's condition requires resettlement in five days; Urgent – where a refugee's condition requires attention before non-urgent cases; and Normal.[39]

Significant effort has been invested in recent years, especially by the United States and Canada, on the development of more responsive emergency resettlement procedures. One reason why the United States and Canada may have taken the lead on this question is because their programmes have previously been criticised for being unresponsive to emergency resettlement needs for a single structural reason.

Given the requirement of adjudication by an official pursuant to a direct interview, the United States, Canada, and Australia must conduct resettlement selection missions to countries of asylum. This creates two difficulties. First, resettlement missions are not responsive to urgent resettlement need as they occur infrequently. Second, for security reasons, selection missions often cannot travel to remote and insecure regions. As a result, refugees in accessible and secure locations are typically favoured. In comparison, European resettlement countries select resettlement candidates through both resettlement missions and on the basis of dossier considerations. Through dossier selection procedures, the urgent resettlement needs of refugees, especially those located in insecure locations inaccessible to selection missions, can be more easily addressed.

The working solution being considered by the United States and Canada for emergency cases, especially in Africa, is the possibility of evacuating the resettlement candidate to a safe house or regional processing centre where the refugee can be accessed by a visa officer, and remain safely until a decision is taken. The implementation of these programmes has, however, been problematic.

The Home Office background paper states that the UK intends to interview all applicants for resettlement, rather than consider applications on a dossier basis.[40] This has a number of benefits, most importantly the development of a greater familiarity with individual cases, which would facilitate the eventual process of reception and integration. In the interest of ensuring that resettlement is an effective and responsive tool of protection, however, provisions should be made in the UK programme to rapidly and effectively respond to emergency and urgent resettlement need. To best ensure that the protection function of resettlement is met, and within the context of the options presented in the Home Office background paper, the permanent secondment of staff to a "hub area" would be one possible way of ensuring that urgent resettlement needs are effectively addressed.[41]

---

36   UNHCR, *New Directions for Resettlement Policy and Practice*, Standing Committee 21st Meeting, EC/51/SC/INF.2, 14 June 2001, paragraph 10.
37   Home Office Research and Statistics Directorate, *Background Paper on UK Quota Resettlement Programme*, prepared for *Listening to the evidence: the future of UK resettlement Policy*, London, 6 February 2003.
38   For a more detailed discussion of these questions, see: UNHCR, Resettlement Section, *Report: Regional Resettlement Workshop*, Addis Ababa, Ethiopia, 27 February–2 March 2001.
39   UNHCR Resettlement Handbook (updated July 2002), V/33.
40   Home Office Research and Statistics Directorate, *Background Paper*, February 2003, paragraph 18.
41   *Ibid.*

The second question that needs to be considered under the protection function of resettlement is, how should the status of individuals be balanced against their need for resettlement?

The core protection function of resettlement may be difficult to achieve in cases of mass influx, in situations where refugees benefit from only *prima facie* refugee status, or where a refugee is recognised only under the Mandate of UNHCR.[42] There are currently two elements to identifying a refugee in need of resettlement. The first is the identification of that individual as a refugee and in need of international protection, as described in Chapter 3 of the Resettlement Handbook. The second is the identification of that refugee as being in need of resettlement according to the criteria outlined in Chapter 4 of the Handbook.

The primary focus of resettlement should be to address the protection needs of vulnerable refugees who – as a result of threats to their life, liberty, and personal security – cannot remain in their country of first asylum and cannot return to their country of origin. Both aspects must be taken into consideration. But not all refugees in need of resettlement will meet the strict refugee definition of the 1951 Refugee Convention. This is especially true in the African context where refugee status may be granted according to the broader parameters of the OAU Convention,[43] and where refugees may have fled a situation of generalised violence, not individual persecution. In such cases, the strength of the refugee claim should be balanced against vulnerability to determine resettlement eligibility and need.

An alarming number of vulnerable refugees have been found not to be eligible for resettlement because they could not demonstrate an individual fear of persecution, but who faced threats to their life and liberty in their country of asylum, and who would face similar threats if returned to their country of origin. In response to this situation, UNHCR has argued that a flexible and protection-based approach to resettlement is "particularly important for refugees who have been in limbo for many years, or for refugees from within *prima facie* populations who have particularly pressing protection needs in the country of asylum even while they may not, at that point in time, fulfill all the requirements of the 1951 Convention definition".[44]

This balance is especially important when considering the eligibility for resettlement of refugee women-at-risk. Under US law, for example, officers of the Immigration and Naturalization Service (INS) are required to conduct refugee status determination (RSD) interviews to ensure that applicants meet the 1951 Convention definition and thereby qualify for refugee admission, but are not directed by law to accord any particular weight to conditions in countries of asylum. In many places, refugee women often have difficulty establishing individual refugee claims based on a narrowly interpreted persecution standard. Often, they are part of larger groups fleeing generalised violence in their country of origin. The main reason they are at risk is often because of their high level of vulnerability in the *country of first asylum*, but the INS officers' attention is directed away from examining those threats because of their concentration on finding specific and explicit grounding of the underlying refugee claim in political, religious, or ethnic persecution of the individual refugee woman in the *country of origin*.

For the protection function of resettlement to be effectively realised, considerations of the status of the individuals' needs to be balanced with their vulnerability in the country of asylum and their need for

---

42   See: UNHCR Resettlement Handbook (revised July 2002), Chapter 3.
43   Article 1(2) of the 1969 Organisation of African Unity (OAU) Convention Governing the Specific Aspects of Refugee Problems in Africa states that in addition to the refugee definition contained in Article 1A(2) of the 1951 Convention relating to the Status of Refugees, "the term 'refugee' shall also apply to every person who, owing to external aggression, occupation, foreign domination or events seriously disturbing public order in either part or the whole of his country of origin or nationality, is compelled to leave his place of habitual residence in order to seek refuge in another place outside his country of origin or nationality".
44   UNHCR, *New Directions for Resettlement Policy and Practice*, Standing Committee 21st Meeting, EC/51/SC/INF.2, 14 June 2001, paragraph 10.

resettlement. The question of how to strike a balance between these two considerations has been recently addressed by the Resettlement Working Group, and the UK programme should include a provision, highlighting the need to apply flexible criteria in appropriate situations and to place specific emphasis on the protection needs of refugees in their country of first asylum, in addition to their inability to return to their country of origin.

Resettlement is a durable solution for protracted refugee situations

Of all the criteria contained in Chapter 4 of the Resettlement Handbook, the 8th criteria, resettlement for refugees without local integration prospects, is by far the most difficult to operationalise.[45] Building from the old notion of resettlement for 'long-stayers', this criteria is to be applied for an individual refugee, or groups of refugees, for whom both local integration, in a manner appropriate to their culture, social, religious, or educational backgrounds, and voluntary repatriation are deemed not to be viable durable solutions in the medium- to long-term. In this way, as argued by UNHCR, "resettlement addresses the need to reinstate national protection, to restore basic dignity and safety, and to secure a future where refugees can enjoy life again".[46]

There is a growing recognition within the policy discussions that resettlement is most effective when it is approached not independently, as an act of rescue for an individual refugee, but as part of a broader protection and durable solution strategy. It is generally recognised that resettlement alone can only provide a durable solution for a very limited number of refugees. In contrast, developing the complementary nature of the three durable solutions, and using resettlement as part of a comprehensive response to particular groups and as a means of engaging the country of asylum on the question of local solutions, is seen as the best use of resettlement.[47]

The Background paper from the Home Office outlined that the initial programme would target one or two geographic regions.[48] If this is the approach the government adopts, it would be most effective to consider how the relatively small annual quota might be used strategically to advance a comprehensive durable solutions strategy for the remaining refugee population. Particular focus could be placed on engaging the country of first asylum on the question of local solutions for those refugees not resettled.[49]

Resettlement is an expression of international solidarity with countries of first asylum

Related to the last point, policy discussions, especially in the past two years, have highlighted the use of resettlement to enhance asylum and protection prospects for those refugees not resettled.[50] Mindful of the various burdens borne by countries of first asylum, it has been argued, especially by UNHCR, that "resettlement can be a particularly useful responsibility-sharing mechanism where there are groups of refugees whose presence in a country of asylum may pose problems for security or other reasons particular to that country."[51]

45 See: UNHCR Resettlement Handbook (revised 2002), IV/31.
46 UNHCR, *Background Note for the Agenda Item: The Use of Resettlement to Address Durable Solutions Needs*, Annual Tripartite Consultations on Resettlement, Geneva, 20–21 June 2001.
47 See: UNHCR, *Strengthening and Expanding Resettlement Today: Dilemmas, Challenges and Opportunities*, Global Consultations on International Protection, Third Track, Fourth Meeting, EC/GC/02/7, 25 April 2002.
48 Home Office Research and Statistics Directorate, *Background Paper*, February 2003, paragraph 17.
49 See: John Fredriksson, *Revitalizing Resettlement as a Durable Solution* in World Refugee Survey 1997, Washington DC: US Committee for Refugees, 1997. While the notion of the complimentary nature of the three durable solutions was central to many discussions during the recent Global Consultations on International Protection, the means of developing such an approach remains unclear. Additional research is urgently required to better understand both how resettlement can serve as part of a comprehensive solution to a refugee situation and how the strategic use of resettlement can enhance asylum.
50 UNHCR, *Background Note for the Agenda Item: Strategic Utilisation of Resettlement to Enhance Asylum and Protection Prospects*, Annual Tripartite Consultations on Resettlement, Geneva, 20 – 21 June 2001.
51 UNHCR, *New Directions for Resettlement Policy and Practice*, Standing Committee 21st Meeting, EC/51/SC/INF.2, 14 June 2001, paragraph 8.

Resettlement may be used as a 'safety-valve' to relieve the pressures faced by countries of first asylum. By demonstrating their solidarity with countries of first asylum through the resettlement of refugees, resettlement countries may contribute to ensuring that the principle of asylum is maintained for those refugees not resettled. At the same time, however, any demonstration of solidarity should be both international and genuine. As the British Refugee Council has argued, "the number and type of refugees the UK undertakes to resettle must demonstrate a real commitment to sharing a global responsibility that falls disproportionately on the shoulders of developing countries".[52]

It is also in this light that the key question facing the development of the UK programme, how to maximise the protection benefits of the limited resources available for resettlement, should be addressed. Approaching resettlement as a question of international solidarity would help ensure that the UK programme could derive maximum protection benefit from the initial quota of 500.

All resettlement programmes should be viewed as part of a global effort to realise the spirit of international solidarity and burden sharing articulated in the preamble of the 1951 Convention. As such, for reasons of principle and pragmatism, the UK would do well not to approach its resettlement programme as an individual effort, but as a component in a larger, global, tripartite resettlement effort.

UNHCR Field Offices are now required to undertake an annual exercise of mapping resettlement need and to identify the resources, both human and material, they require to meet those needs.[53] These needs, along with profiles of populations in need of resettlement, will then be reported to the Annual Tripartite Consultations on Resettlement. It is on this basis that, in consultation with other resettlement partners, the UK may determine where its quota of 500 will have the greatest impact. Resettlement priorities set in this way will ensure the maximisation of the protection benefits of a limited quota and ensure that resettlement activities are a true expression of solidarity.

Finally, true involvement in global resettlement efforts should mean that resettlement countries, like the UK, are engaged in all aspects of resettlement and protection work, not simply in the consideration of refugees referred for resettlement. As a committed resettlement partner, it is essential to demonstrate support for the resettlement process by addressing the current constraints at the field level and by understanding the preconditions required for effective resettlement.

There is a prevailing feeling of frustration with resettlement processing in regions of refugee origin where the UK intends to select candidates for resettlement. Refugees are frustrated that the resettlement process remains shrouded in mystery and that there is typically insufficient support from UNHCR to guide them through the process and support them while they await a decision.

NGOs are frustrated at the lack of transparency and support during the UNHCR resettlement-referral process. NGOs feel that they are often unable to guide refugees through the process due to a lack of information on the resettlement process, that they experience difficulties referring needy cases to UNHCR for resettlement consideration, and that UNHCR appears to be consistently unsympathetic to the material needs of asylum seekers awaiting a decision.

Resettlement countries – especially the United States, Canada, and Australia – are frustrated that UNHCR is consistently unable to provide sufficient cases to meet resettlement quotas, and that the quality of the referrals received falls below the minimum standards of the resettlement countries.

52   (British) Refugee Council, *Principles for a UK Resettlement Programme*, London: March 2002.
53   See: UNHCR Resettlement Handbook (revised 2002), Chapter 7.

In response to these frustrations, the best way to improve processing is by identifying and addressing two current constraints on processing in the field: programme constraints and resource constraints.[54]

Programme constraints: There is currently a significant discrepancy between the number of refugees eligible for resettlement and the number of resettlement places available. According to the 8th resettlement criteria (outlined above), the overwhelming majority of refugees in protracted refugee situations, numbering millions, would be eligible for resettlement. Yet, under current quotas, less than one per cent of refugees world-wide will be resettled in a given year.

This leads to a tension between eligibility, on the one hand, and prioritisation on the other. While a refugee may be eligible for resettlement, the limited number of resettlement opportunities results in the necessity to prioritise resettlement need. UNHCR's field practices state that resettlement prioritisation should be according to vulnerability, but even this consideration would lead to a pool of refugees eligible for resettlement that far exceeds the resettlement quota. In reality, this leads to the notion of a resettlement queue, and to great emphasis being placed by refugees on their place in the queue.

Once this point has been reached, objective criteria become difficult to apply and demand, desperation and uncertainty continue to increase. It is in this environment that the opportunities for the type of fraud and mismanagement experienced in Nairobi multiply[55] and where all means to 'jump the queue' will be considered by desperate refugees. This lack of opportunity, coupled with desperation, can lead vulnerable refugees who would be eligible for resettlement to seek alternative means of escape. Increasingly, the most common alternative is smuggling.

In this light, delegates to the 2001 Annual Tripartite Consultations on Resettlement encouraged the expansion of resettlement in the European Union, both individually and collectively. UNHCR stated that: "The possibility of creating additional resettlement opportunities, as a particular mechanism to share responsibilities with countries of refuge, should be encouraged and further explored. Resettlement is one of the tools in the arsenal of protection within the whole governance structure for refugees. A fresh look should be taken at the useful role that fair and global resettlement quotas might play in helping to realise a world of law and in giving practical meaning to the need to offer durable solutions to refugees under the UNHCR mandate."[56]

These policy discussions culminated in EXCOM Conclusion on International Protection (No. 90 (LII) – 2001), which specifically highlighted the need to expand resettlement opportunities. While emphasising the fundamental importance of durable solutions and commending States that facilitate these solutions, the Conclusion encouraged "initiatives directed at diversifying resettlement opportunities by increasing the number of resettlement countries, thereby sharing resettlement needs more widely, and meeting increased resettlement needs".[57]

By announcing an annual resettlement quota, the UK has taken a tangible step in addressing the resource constraint. It must, however, be recognised that the proposed quota of 500 is very limited. To more fully address the resource constraint, the UK would do well to consider increasing its annual quota and encourage European non-resettlement states to also develop resettlement programmes.

---

54   For more consideration on the resource implications of increased resettlement activities, see: Gary Troeller, *Opinion: UNHCR Resettlement: Evolution and Future Direction, International Journal of Refugee Law,* Vol. 14, no. 1, 2002.
55   See: UNHCR Press release: *UNHCR receives report on Nairobi investigation,* 25 January 2001, http://www.unhcr.ch
56   *Background Note for the Agenda Item: Strategic Utilization of Resettlement to Enhance Asylum and Protection Prospects,* Annual Tripartite Consultations on Resettlement, Geneva, 20 June 2001, paragraph 20.
57   UNHCR, EXCOM, Conclusion on International Protection (No. 90 (LII)–2001).

Resource constraints: The increasing limitation of the essential resources required to identify and process refugees in need of resettlement places a significant constraint on the system as a whole. The identification of refugees in need of resettlement and the preparation of a dossier for submission to a resettlement country is a remarkably time-consuming task. In the absence of early registration and individual refugee status determination, it has been estimated that an average of 8–10 hours is required per resettlement submission. When these time constraints are viewed in light of recent funding cut-backs to UNHCR, which have resulted in the posting of very few UNHCR Resettlement Officers in regions with large and protracted refugee populations, the implications of the resource constraint are clear. There are too few officers with exclusive resettlement responsibilities posted in complex situations facing overwhelming resettlement need.

In response to this acute human resource constraint, UNHCR and resettlement countries have considered a number of short-term and flexible remedies. The Canadian government, for example, agreed to the secondment of two senior immigration officials to UNHCR resettlement activities in East Africa and the Middle East. Recent emphasis has also been placed on developing the UNHCR–ICMC Resettlement Deployment Scheme, a programme to support the interviewing of refugees for resettlement through the deployment of NGO staff to UNHCR offices around the world for periods ranging from three to 12 months. In 2001, the Scheme deployed a total of 50 people to 32 locations in 28 different countries.[58]

While secondees and deployees cannot replace UNHCR Resettlement Officers, such creative means of addressing the human resources constraint must be explored, while also exploring how the on-going resettlement activities of UNHCR may be more effectively and predictably supported by donor countries. If the UK is to rely on UNHCR for the identification and referral of resettlement cases, thought must be given to the human and material support the UNHCR will require to fulfil this function.

The direct consequence of these human and material resource constraints required to conduct processing in the regions is a significant backlog of unexamined cases and long waiting periods for the results of interviews. Lengthy resettlement procedures have left vulnerable refugees stranded in desperate conditions for months on end, often with little or no assistance from UNHCR. Recent funding cut-backs have directly impeded not only UNHCR's ability to exercise its protection mandate in many regions, but have also resulted in a reduction of the levels of assistance provided to asylum seekers and refugees as they await decisions on their asylum or resettlement applications.

Resettlement activities can also lead to high expectations within refugee populations, which places additional strains on resettlement staff, and may result in concerns relating to their personal safety and security. In the absence of reliable, credible and consistent information, refugees not only become frustrated, but susceptible to misinformation and manipulation. Resettlement countries need to be full partners, along with UNHCR and NGOs, in ensuring that they are providing complete and accessible information on resettlement which helps manage resettlement expectations. Information should be provided on the meaning and nature of resettlement, the resettlement process, resettlement criteria, the roles of the various resettlement partners, and whether it is possible to request resettlement.

Making such information widely available to refugees would also serve to reduce the instances of fraud and corruption in the resettlement process. Concerns relating to levels of fraud and corruption in the resettlement process have been growing in recent years, especially since the recent corruption scandal in Nairobi.[59] The

---

58   For more information on the ICMC–UNHCR Resettlement Deployment Scheme, see: http://www.icmc.net
59   See: UNHCR Press Release: "UNHCR receives report on Nairobi investigation", 25 January 2001. Available on-line: http://www.unhcr.ch

dramatic growth in resettlement activities in recent years has not been coupled with corresponding increases in staffing or corresponding developments in management and oversight of resettlement activities. As a consequence, resettlement activities in various regions have been plagued by allegations of fraud and mismanagement. To this end, EXCOM Conclusion on International Protection (No. 90 (LII) – 2001) urged "further UNHCR efforts to ensure the integrity of the processing of the resettlement caseload" and encouraged "States and UNHCR to continue to pursue a strategic and systematic approach to the problem of attempted fraud or other abuse."

In light of these concerns, resettlement countries, NGOs, and UNHCR developed new guidelines on the processing of resettlement cases in field locations and the management of resettlement activities. These guidelines were approved following the 2002 ATC and were incorporated into the *Resettlement Handbook* as new Chapters 5 (Basic Procedures) and 7 (Management). While these guidelines will help reduce instances of resettlement fraud and add credibility to UNHCR's resettlement activities, the implementation of these guidelines will place additional demands on resettlement staff in field offices who are already overburdened. Support is therefore required to ensure that the resources are available in every field office engaged in resettlement activities to ensure that effective procedures are in place to reduce the chances of fraud and corruption in the resettlement process.

Finally, many of the concerns about the resource and time-intensive nature of resettlement, in addition to concerns about fraud and corruption in the process, can be addressed by ensuring that certain preconditions for resettlement activities are in place. The most important pre-condition is a full and effective registration process, detailing family composition, undertaken and maintained in a non-resettlement context.

The misuse of resettlement

The central role of resettlement in Australia's new approach to asylum seekers,[60] has brought the independence of resettlement into doubt and has, for some, recast resettlement as a tool of migration management and not a tool of international protection. As argued by UNHCR, "while resettlement constitutes a multi-faceted response mechanism, it is certainly not the panacea for all problems besetting asylum systems today, particularly those related to widespread illegal migration".[61] UNHCR develops this position by arguing that:

> Resettlement and asylum are two distinct and separate possibilities. It is therefore critical to the integrity of the international protection system that resettlement processing and the promotion of asylum are pursued in tandem, and not used to work against each other... Resettlement is only one available tool of protection within the whole international refugee protection regime. Using resettlement to further restrict the admission of individual asylum seekers would undermine the right to seek asylum, which is anchored in the Universal Declaration of Human Rights, and is at the very core of the protection regime for refugees. Resettlement must continue to function as a complement to other protection activities and durable solutions. It is not a substitute for the right to seek and enjoy asylum.[62]

60 See: US Committee for Refugees, *Sea Change: Australia's new approach to asylum seekers*, February 2002. Available on-line: http://www.refugees.org
61 UNHCR, *New Directions for Resettlement Policy and Practice*, Standing Committee 21st Meeting, EC/51/SC/INF.2, 14 June 2001, paragraph 23.
62 UNHCR, *New Directions for Resettlement Policy and Practice*, Standing Committee 21st Meeting, EC/51/SC/INF.2, 14 June 2001, paragraph 24.

To this end, refugee advocates should be encouraged by the fact that the February 2002 Government White Paper[63] clearly states that the resettlement programme will be additional to current asylum procedures. Serious attention should, however, be paid to what a resettlement programme can do for the public perception of refugees. Managed well, a resettlement programme could foster wider public support for all refugees. Managed poorly, a resettlement programme may result in a public perception of asylum seekers as queue-jumpers, as we have seen in Australia.

Conclusion

Resettlement has historically played an important role in comprehensive responses to refugee situations. Highlighted most dramatically by the resettlement efforts associated with the World Refugee Year in 1960 and the CPA, resettlement has been most effective when employed as a strategic complement to other efforts to address the causes of flight, conditions in countries of asylum, and the pursuit of other durable solutions. This recognition has been reinforced by recent discussion between the Tripartite resettlement partners, and has led to the emergence of international resettlement policy.

Managed well, resettlement works. It is a valuable instrument in the international protection tool-box and often the only means of ensuring the protection of refugees who cannot remain in their country of first asylum and cannot return to their country of origin. In such cases, resettlement is not the least preferred solution; it is the only solution. Tens of thousands of refugees, who would otherwise be at risk in their country of first asylum or even *refouled* to their country of origin, receive international protection through resettlement every year.

Resettlement is a tool of international protection, a durable solution for refugees and an expression of international solidarity with countries of first asylum. Applying these principles, as articulated in recent international resettlement policy discussions, would help ensure the successful implementation and development of the UK resettlement programme.

---

63   UK Home Office, *Secure Borders, Safe Haven: Integration with Diversity in Modern Britain*, UK Government White Paper, February 2002. See also: Response from (British) Refugee Council. http://www.refugeecouncil.org.uk/

Background papers

7. Asylum and Appeals Policy Directorate (AAPD), Home Office

UK quota resettlement programme

This background paper represents current thinking and our working assumptions for the development of the quota resettlement programme. Many of the issues have yet to be finally decided upon.

We are developing the quota resettlement programme as part of our commitment to help develop an effective international protection system. In the White Paper *Secure Borders, Safe Haven* we proposed developing ways in which those refugees whose lives cannot be protected in their region of origin could have their claim considered before they reach the UK, then travel here in safety and receive protection.

Our objectives in providing resettlement are to:

- provide a sustainable and long-term solution to those refugees whose lives, liberty, or other fundamental human rights are at risk where they are living;
- remove from those most vulnerable refugees a perceived need to seek the services of a people smuggler if they want to reach the UK; and
- contribute to solving any regional need for asylum.

The resettlement programme will operate in addition to current asylum determination procedures. It will be operated in conjunction with UNHCR, along with other non-government bodies. The aim in the first year of operation will be to resettle 500 people.

Background

The UK currently operates two informal resettlement schemes: the Mandate Refugee scheme and the Ten or More plan. However, resettlement under these programmes is limited; for the Mandate Refugee scheme applicants must have close ties in the UK; and for the Ten or More plan, applicants must show that they require medical attention that is not available where they are living.

Applications from refugees for resettlement under the Mandate Refugee scheme are referred to the UK by UNHCR. They are received by the British Red Cross, who contact the applicant's family, and conduct an initial sift of cases. The Home Office then considers each case, with the British Red Cross arranging travel to the UK if successful. On arrival, the applicant's reception and integration needs are met by their families.

We have not yet decided whether to merge the Mandate Refugee Programme, or the Ten or More Plan, with the quota programme. Much of this will depend on the numbers of refugees currently coming to the UK under those schemes. For the first year, we are working on the assumption that the quota programme will be separate.

The UK also has provided resettlement in response to emergency situations since the end of the Second World War, in particular:

- 140,000 Polish military exiles resettled here after 1940;
- over 28,000 Ugandan Asians resettled here in the early 1970's;
- 3,000 Chilean refugees resettled here in the late 1970's;
- approximately 20,000 Vietnamese resettled here between 1979 and 1982;
- over 2,500 Bosnians resettled here in the early 1990's; and
- over 4,000 Kosovans participated in the Humanitarian Evacuation Programme in the late 1990's (although most received temporary status).

However, we want to provide a permanent and broader resettlement route to the UK for those refugees whose protection cannot be safeguarded where they are living, with appropriate assistance and support available to people arriving in the UK via a resettlement routes.

This type of general resettlement programme is well established in many countries.

Country	Resettlement quota in 2000	Year programme established
Denmark	500	1989
Netherlands	500	1984
Finland	700	1979
New Zealand	750	1979
Norway	1,481 (though recently reduced to 750 per year because of a higher number of asylum cases)	Not known
Sweden	1,840	1950
Australia	8,000	1947
Canada	11,000	1978
USA	73,000	1980

Development of the quota programme

The key question for us in developing the programme's detail is how best to balance the many demands on resources for resettlement: how can we most effectively provide protection to those who need it; and what should our priorities be taking into account their impacts on the programme?

We aim to start the quota programme in April 2003, and to resettle 500 people per year. We hope to be ready to begin considering applications in April, with actual arrivals taking place later in the year. It is our working assumption that in later years the quota would increase, but in determining its size, we would take into account resources available and any pressures on local services.

We are also working on the assumption that the provision of services for resettlement will be contracted-out in the main, with the Home Office's focus on the qualitative decision and management of the policy and process.

Consideration of applications

The Home Office, working with UNHCR, would set criteria for resettlement to the UK. In addition, we would map any practical considerations faced (for example, shortages of particular types of accommodation) which may affect the types of cases that could be considered. The criteria and practical constraints would be reviewed as necessary.

UNHCR annually assesses the global need for resettlement. This highlights where the need for resettlement arises most acutely, and whether there were particular nationalities or social groups for whom a resettlement need is high.

Having set the programme's quota, we would then ask UNHCR to refer to us cases they considered might be suitable for resettlement. IND caseworkers would then consider applications until the quota was met. This determination process would include interviewing all candidates. We have yet to decide what health and security screening applicants and their dependants would be required to complete. On successful completion of these phases (referral, consideration, screening, and final determination) we envisage that some form of counselling or orientation/information would be provided to brief applicants on what to expect of resettlement to the UK. Finally, arrangements would be made for their departure and reception.

The UK will make the final decision in each case. However, if there were a disagreement between UNHCR and the UK caseworker regarding a particular case, both officials would discuss the case in detail in order to understand fully each other's concerns. Refused cases would be reviewed if new factors came to light.

For the programme's first year, our desire is to take a simple approach by focusing on more straightforward cases and in one or two geographical areas, in order that our processes can be fully tested.

Interviewing applicants

We intend to interview all applicants for resettlement, rather than consider applications on a dossier basis. Given our desire to operate from one or two hub areas in the programme's first year, our options for conducting interviews are:

- for caseworkers to conduct missions lasting a few days or weeks to a specific area;
- to permanently second staff to a hub area solely to conduct interviewing, and manage the process in-country; or
- to appoint staff who would act as a roving resettlement officer, spending most of their time travelling around the hub areas conducting interviews, but not based exclusively in any one area.

Criteria

We are working on the assumption that we will be using UNHCR's criteria for resettlement, but that given the very large numbers of people in need of resettlement (which surpasses the number of places available) we also need to establish UK-specific sifting criteria. These may reflect practical considerations relating to our capacity, and the new nature of the scheme (and therefore our desire to start with a reasonably straightforward approach), and they may reflect principles linked to existing policies within IND.

Examples of the practical considerations we will want to take account of are:

- the type of accommodation available in the UK;
- the availability of specialist medical treatment; and
- the readiness of our processes, and support, for refugees who require a higher level of support.

Those issues falling somewhere between are:

- the priorities of the programme regarding the most effective use of resources; and
- whether we have a target for particularly vulnerable groups, such as women at risk.

Examples of existing IND policies that *might* have a read-across to resettlement include:

- family reunification;
- the existence of routes for resettlement for those with close ties, etc;
- revocation of leave to remain in cases of serious criminal behaviour by refugees;
- arrangements for the sponsorship of elderly relatives; and
- access to medical treatment.

Integration support

We think that refugees who are resettled to the UK are likely to need some additional, or different, services or information to those people who have claimed asylum in the UK. Resettled refugees will not, for example, have been through the process of induction, or provided with financial support or accommodation. They may have arrived with few or no possessions, or without suitable clothing for UK weather, and some may have been traumatised by the circumstances necessitating their resettlement.

Location of settlement areas

Evaluations of previous resettlement programmes have pointed to the need to support integration of resettled refuges in determining the location of permanent accommodation by taking into account:

- housing availability (for reception and in the longer term);
- availability of work (ideally at varying levels);
- ratio of refugees to resident population;
- presence of refugee support networks;
- established ethnic minority communities;
- preference of refugee;
- prevalence of racially motivated violence; and
- 'local knowledge' issues.

Both before and after arrival we want to provide assistance that will help to facilitate successful settlement in the UK. At present, we think that the support provided should include the provision of accommodation, counselling, orientation advice on how to access services like education and health, and help with essential items for day-to-day living. Our working assumption is that this assistance on arrival would be provided by a range of organisations, but funded and overseen by the Home Office.

We see four points at which integration support will be needed:

- pre-departure, in the form of information about the process and life in the UK;
- welcome on arrival;
- reception accommodation (unless placed direct into their long term accommodation), induction and services; and
- move-on into long-term accommodation/mid-long term support.

Pre-departure

We want to ensure that refugees who are to be resettled to the UK understand what is going to happen, and when, and that they are provided with information that will help them prepare for their move, both practically and psychologically. We want to ensure that the refugees have an accurate picture of what resettlement to the UK will mean for them. We need to understand what information the refugees will need, and in what medium will be most useful for them to receive it.

Welcome

Resettled refugees will need to be met and welcomed on arrival, and transported to their reception accommodation. Where the arriving person is coming to the UK to join family, we hope that this could involve them.

Reception

In the resettled person's first few weeks or months in the UK, they may need to receive:

- paperwork and documentation that will be needed (National Insurance Number, etc);
- financial support (this will depend on benefit entitlements and how we link into benefit system);
- interpreting and translation services;
- induction/familiarisation information (how to contact the police, doctor, school, responsibilities as a citizen, using sterling, accessing social support, etc);
- counselling/health treatment if needed;
- support and assistance in choosing where to live/registering children in education/accessing medical services;
- language lessons; and
- skills audit/employment advice/re-accreditation.

The type of reception accommodation opted for will depend on the throughput of arrivals and also on the accommodation that is available. Models include providing a reception centre, self-contained accommodation with common services, other accommodation that is removed from the site of support services, etc.

Move-on

We do not know yet how long resettled people will remain in reception accommodation, or what the arrangements will be for move-on into permanent housing.

In coming months we will need to establish:

- what, if any, on-going support is needed in addition to mainstream services; and
- where are the most appropriate areas for resettlement of the quota refugees (if this is likely to be different from the reception area).

If you wish to discuss the development of the quota programme in more detail, please contact (preferably by email):

Pre-arrival issues:
Claire Downie
International Asylum Policy Unit
Tel: 020 8760 8476
Email: claire.downie@homeoffice.gsi.gov.uk

Reception and integration issues:
Penny Hart
Refugee Integration Unit
Tel: 020 8760 8408
Email: penny.hart@homeoffice.gsi.gov.uk

International Asylum Policy Unit
February 2003

8.
Research Division, International Organization for Migration (IOM)

Global trends in resettlement: comparing the UK with other countries

Background Paper prepared for the Home Office Research Seminar on Refugee Resettlement held on February 6, 2003, London[64]

This brief paper provides a presentation of global trends in resettlement for the years 2000 and 2001 based on data collected by the International Organization for Migration (IOM). The main purpose of the paper is to compare the UK with other countries, in terms of the number of persons being resettled and their profile. This paper provides an overview of IOM-facilitated resettlement movements in 2000 and 2001.

International comparisons with countries such as the US, Canada, Norway, and Sweden that have a longer history in operating refugee resettlement programmes, may be useful in helping to inform policy makers in the UK as they prepare to expand current provisions for resettlement.

IOM data on resettlement are derived from IOM operational programmes under which refugees and their accompanying family members are offered transportation and other resettlement assistance, or in the context of family reunification programmes once they have been settled. In the latter event, family members are either admitted under migrant resettlement or regular immigration (family reunion) schemes of the recipient countries. IOM provides resettlement services through its 165 offices world-wide. Available IOM data record: 1) place of departure/arrival; 2) nationality; 3) age and sex; 4) family structure and, 5) civil status of the persons resettled under IOM programmes. Such data include Convention refugees who are covered under UNHCR referrals, other refugees who are admitted directly by recipient countries (without UNHCR referral), and persons destined for family reunification. IOM data include a wide range of persons being resettled.

During 2001, IOM resettled a total of 87,380 persons. During that same period, some 33,100 refugees were resettled from countries of first asylum under UNHCR auspices.[65]

---

64   Prepared by Frank Laczko, flaczko@iom.int, and Aiko Kikkawa, akikkawa@iom.int, Research and Publications Division, IOM. A comprehensive analysis on IOM resettlement was submitted to Migration Policy Institute Roundtable on Resettlement Programmes Brussels, 5 November 2002.
65   UNCHR (2002) *Statistical Yearbook 2001*, October 2002, UNHCR, Geneva.

Global resettlement and the UK, 2000-2001

Summary

In 2000 and 2001, 429 and 420 refugees respectively, and their family members were resettled in the UK. The UK ranks as the tenth-largest resettlement country and represents 0.44 per cent of the IOM resettlement caseload globally, and 3.3 per cent within Europe.

Numbering 340, Somali nationals represented the largest group of resettled persons in the UK and accounted for 40 per cent of the entire resettlement caseload. The majority of them arrived from two countries of asylum, Ethiopia (69%) and Kenya (23%). Globally, Somalis ranked fourth among all resettled national groups.

The UK hosts the largest group of single persons (78%) compared with the global average of 60 per cent. This may be expected to have some impact on subsequent family reunification, and the integration patterns in the host societies.

In terms of gender, the male/female ratio in the UK stood at 0.49/0.51, compared with a global ratio of 0.51/0.49. As to age distribution, nearly 40 per cent of resettled persons were between the ages of 10 to 19.

Total resettlement: 2000 and 2001 (Tables 1 and 2)

According to IOM data, in 2000 and 2001 the UK hosted 429 and 420 refugees and their family members respectively, through various resettlement programmes. IOM programmes facilitated these resettlement movements. A very limited number of refugees with severe medical conditions are resettled each year through the Ten or More Plan. Refugees are also resettled under the UNHCR Mandate scheme. These programmes are likely to account for the major part of the refugees resettled in the UK, although it should be noted that it is not possible to distinguish arrivals according to programme from IOM data at this time. Furthermore, it is possible that some of the arrivals may have taken place through other IOM-facilitated resettlement movements.

In 2000 and 2001, the total number of resettlements in the UK stood at 849, representing 0.44 per cent of the total global resettlement facilitated by IOM. The US was by far the most important country of resettlement, receiving 134,391 persons, or 69.7 per cent, followed by Canada with 23,098 persons (12%). In the wake of the September 11 attacks, the volume of refugee resettlement to the US registered a significant drop. The intake by Nordic countries also fell in 2001.

In Europe, the three largest countries of resettlement were Denmark, Norway, and Sweden with a combined total of nearly 70 per cent of all resettlements in Europe. In 2000, for example, Norway set an annual quota for refugees (excluding family members) of 1,500, Sweden of 1,375, and Denmark of around 500.[66] The UK for its part, accounted for around 3.3 per cent of total resettlement to the region.

---

66 UNCHCR (2001) *Easy Guide to Refugee Resettlement Programmes*, UNHCR, Geneva.
The reason why IOM figures are higher than the annual quota is that IOM figures also include the family members accompanying or reuniting with, refugees.

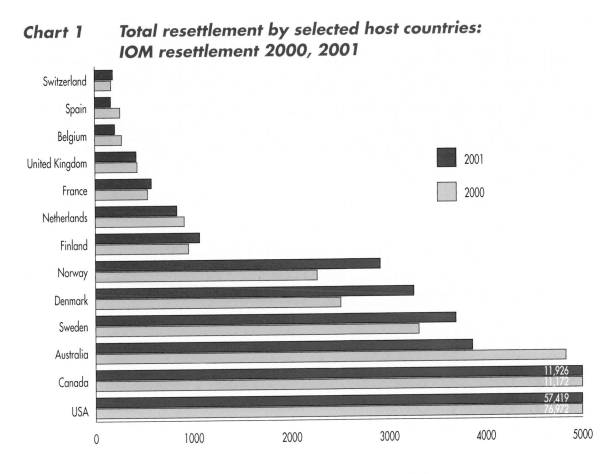

Chart 1   Total resettlement by selected host countries: IOM resettlement 2000, 2001

Resettled refugees by nationality and country of departure (Tables 3 and 4)

As already referred to, with 340 persons, Somalis made up the largest national group of resettled persons to the UK, accounting for 40 per cent of the total. The majority of them came to the UK from two major countries of departure, Ethiopia (69%) and Kenya (23%).

Somalis ranked as the fourth-largest national group to be resettled world-wide by IOM. The largest group was from Bosnia and Herzegovina, but no Bosnians were resettled in the UK during that period. This may be explained by the fact that a number of European countries have received Bosnian refugees not on the basis of resettlement, but under a temporary protection status, allowing refugees to remain for a restricted period of time.

In 2000 and 2001, the UK accepted a total of 174 Iraqis for resettlement, the second-largest national group to be resettled there. The main countries of asylum from where they had arrived included Jordan, Syria, and Lebanon. In 2001, the number of Iraqis increased by 40 per cent from the previous year, which is in contrast to the global trend, which saw the total number of resettled Iraqi nationals decline during the period 2000-2001.

Chart 2   ***Person resettled to the UK by the country of origin: IOM resettlement 2000, 2001***

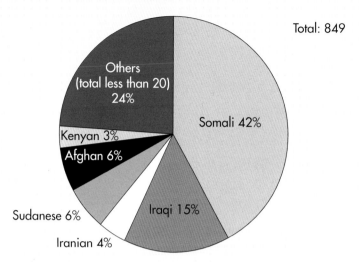

Total: 849

Marital status of resettled persons (Table 5)

The UK hosted more single persons (78%) compared with the global average of 60 per cent. The comparable percentage for the US and Canada is less than 60 per cent, while that for European countries stands above 70 per cent. This may be expected to have some impact on subsequent family reunification and integration patterns.

Age and sex of resettled persons (Table 6)

The gender distribution was fairly balanced, with a slight preponderance of women (0.49/0.51 for the UK vs. 0.51/0.49 globally). An exceptionally large proportion of resettled persons (close to 40%) belonged to the age group of 10–19.

Annexes: Number of resettlements in the UK

Table 1   *Persons resettled by country of destination: IOM resettlement 2000-2001*

Country	2000	2001	Total	%
USA	76,972	57,419	134,391	69.7
Canada	11,172	11,926	23,098	12.0
Australia	4,829	3,860	8,689	4.5
Sweden	3,308	3,691	6,999	3.6
Denmark	2,505	3,257	5,762	3.0
Norway	2,264	2,909	5,173	2.7
Finland	953	1,067	2,020	1.0
Netherlands	910	836	1,746	0.9
France	534	574	1,108	0.6
United Kingdom	**429**	**420**	**849**	**0.4**
Belgium	272	203	475	0.2
Spain	257	162	419	0.2
Switzerland	165	183	348	0.2
Italy	114	204	318	0.2
Japan	139	131	270	0.1
Ireland	181	69	250	0.1
Brazil	58	149	207	0.1
Germany	82	71	153	0.1
Benin	53	79	132	0.1
Austria	29	74	103	0.1
Chile	58	35	93	0.0
Iceland	27	36	63	0.0
New Zealand	32	8	40	0.0
Burkina Faso	20	4	24	0.0
Argentina	6	5	11	0.0
Luxembourg		7	7	0.0
Portugal	1	1	2	0.0
Total	**105,370**	**87,380**	**192,750**	**100.0**

Table 2   Persons resettled in European countries: IOM resettlement 2000-2001

Country	2000	2001	Total	%
Sweden	3,308	3,691	6,999	27.13
Denmark	2,505	3,257	5,762	22.34
Norway	2,264	2,909	5,173	20.05
Finland	953	1,067	2,020	7.83
Netherlands	910	836	1,746	6.77
France	534	574	1,108	4.30
United Kingdom	**429**	**420**	**849**	**3.29**
Belgium	272	203	475	1.84
Spain	257	162	419	1.62
Switzerland	165	183	348	1.35
Italy	114	204	318	1.23
Ireland	181	69	250	0.97
Germany	82	71	153	0.59
Austria	29	74	103	0.40
Iceland	27	36	63	0.24
Luxembourg		7	7	0.03
Portugal	1	1	2	0.01
Total	**12,031**	**13,764**	**25,795**	**100.0**

Table 3   Persons resettled in the UK by country of origin (nationality): IOM resettlement 2000-2001

Country of Origin	2000	2001	Total
Somalia	178	162	340
Iraq	65	108	173
Iran	19	32	51
Sudan	25	18	43
Afghanistan	26	15	41
Kenya	14	14	28
Congo (Zairian)	12	7	19
Ethiopia	11	4	15
Yugoslavia	13		13
Uganda	5	8	13
Sierra Leone	8	5	13
India	8	4	12
Rwanda	10		10
Cameroon	1	5	6
Burundi	1	4	5
Sri Lanka	2	2	4
Azerbaijan		4	4
Vietnam	1	2	3
Togo	3		3
Nigeria		3	3
China		3	3
Kuwait		3	3
Algeria	3		3
Ghana	3		3
Liberia	2		2
Tanzania		2	2
Senegal	2		2
Ivory Coast	1		1
Pakistan	1		1
Colombia		1	1
Jordan		1	1
Croatia	1		1
Undetermined	14	13	27
Total	**429**	**420**	**849**

Table 4   ***Persons resettled in the UK by country of departure: IOM resettlement 2000-2001***

Country of Departure	2000	2001	Total
Ethiopia	121	121	242
Kenya	92	59	151
Jordan	47	42	89
Syria	7	25	32
Uganda	14	10	24
Dem. Rep of Congo	16	7	23
Yemen	5	18	23
Pakistan	18	4	22
Sudan	11	11	22
Turkey	9	13	22
Egypt	12	7	19
Lebanon	13	5	18
Iran	5	11	16
Cyprus	1	12	13
Thailand		13	13
India	2	10	12
Macedonia	12		12
Gambia	8		8
Nigeria		8	8
Austria		6	6
Côte d'Ivoire	6		6
Germany	2	4	6
Ghana	5	1	6
Tanzania	2	4	6
China	1	4	5
Malaysia	5		5
Moldova		5	5
Azerbaijan		4	4
Qatar		4	4
Tunisia	3		3
Congo	2		2
Djibouti		2	2
Netherlands	2		2
Russia		2	2
Senegal		2	2
Ukraine	2		2
Yugoslavia	2		2
Sierra Leone		2	2
Belarus	1		1
Cameroon	1		1
Colombia		1	1
Indonesia		1	1
Kuwait		1	1
Madagascar	1		1
Mozambique	1		1
Nepal		1	1
Total	**429**	**420**	**849**

Table 5 **Persons resettled in the UK by marital status:
IOM resettlement 2000-2001**

	Single	%	Married	%	Widowed	%	No data	Total
USA	76,945	57.3	45,989	34.2	2,215	1.6	9242	134,391
Canada	14,571	63.1	8,330	36.1	186	0.8	11	23,098
Australia	5,056	58.2	3,468	39.9	165	1.9	0	8,689
Sweden	5,117	73.1	1,828	26.1	48	0.7	6	6,999
Denmark	4,392	76.2	1,316	22.8	54	0.9	0	5,762
Norway	3,610	69.8	1,473	28.5	76	1.5	14	5,173
Finland	1,332	65.9	654	32.4	32	1.6	2	2,020
Netherlands	1,316	75.4	413	23.7	11	0.6	6	1,746
France	874	78.9	222	20.0	1	0.1	11	1,108
United Kingdom	**663**	**78.1**	**179**	**21.1**	**2**	**0.2**	**5**	**849**
Spain	257	61.3	162	38.7		0.0		419
Switzerland	252	72.4	92	26.4	2	0.6	2	348

Table 6 **Persons resettled in the UK by family status at the time of
travel: IOM resettlement 2000-2001**

Family status	2000	2001	Total
Head of family, travelling with family	37	30	67
Dependant, travelling with head of family	254	241	495
Dependant, travelling without head of family	83	119	202
Unattached individual	50	30	80
No data	5		5
Total	**429**	**420**	**849**

Table 7 **Persons resettled in the UK by age and sex: IOM resettlement 2000-2001**

Age	Sex	2000	2001	Total
0–9	Female	50	44	94
	Male	–52	–47	99
10–19	Female	73	71	144
	Male	–93	–96	189
20–29	Female	28	31	59
	Male	22	–22	44
30–39	Female	23	30	53
	Male	14	–23	37
40–49	Female	17	19	36
	Male	13	–11	24
50–59	Female	14	8	22
	Male	9	–10	19
60–69	Female	7	4	11
	Male	2	–1	3
70–79	Female	5	2	7
	Male	2	–1	3
No data		5		5
Grand total		**429**	**420**	**849**

Workshops

Workshops provided participants with the opportunity to discuss the content of the presentations and their own knowledge and experiences of the resettlement process. Morning workshops focused on informing preparation for the implementation of the UK resettlement programme in April. Afternoon workshops considered future development of the programme.

Workshop A

Information needs of resettled refugees pre-departure and post-arrival

Facilitators

Verity Gelsthorpe (IRSS) Carolyne Tah (IRSS) Claire Downie (AAPD)

Participants

Kaltun Hassan (RAP)

Anna Reisenberger (Refugee Council)

Gil Loescher (IISS)

Vu Khanh Thanh (An Viet Foundation)

Michael Kingsley-Nynah (UNHCR UK)

Ruben Ahlvin (Swedish Migration Board)

Sorcha O'Callaghan (IRC UK)

Stephanie Dickinson (DWP)

Lauren Herlitz (IRSS)

Amina Hussein (Red Cross)

Sarah Hayward (Employability Forum)

Charles Davy (ICMC)

Wondimu Yohannes (Refugee Action)

Richard Williams (Refugee Council)

Liz Westmorland (Yorkshire & Humberside Consortium)

Peter Ward (IRSS)

Joanne van Selm (MPI)

Matthew Gibney (RSC)

James Milner (RSC)

Helena Ishmael (Horn of Africa Community Group)

Felicity Clarkson (AAPD)

Jan Shaw (Amnesty International)

Vaughan Robinson (University of Wales, Swansea)

Zamila Bunglawala (Strategic Policy Team)

Patrick Collier, (IRSS)

Diane Grammer (IOM)

Furio De Angelis (UNHCR)

Introduction

Information about resettlement can be given to refugees and service providers throughout the resettlement process. The aim of this workshop was to consider the information which could be provided, who could provide it, and how the information could be presented, in order to gather and inform best practice. It was also to consider any differences between resettled refugees and spontaneous asylum seekers (see Appendix 2 for further information).

Does experience point to resettled refugees needing additional or different support to spontaneous refugees post-arrival?

There may be similarities between spontaneous and resettled refugees, particularly with regard to their integration needs. However, key differences in individuals' needs may become apparent once the programme begins. An individual needs assessment could be carried out to identify the specific needs of resettled refugees.

There are noticeable differences in process between resettlement and spontaneous asylum seeking. These include:

- *Asylum status*: resettled refugees will be given refugee status automatically on arrival in the UK, so unlike spontaneous asylum seekers, they will not face a period of uncertainty about the outcome of their asylum case.
- *Manner of arrival*: this will differ markedly from spontaneous asylum seekers. Resettled refugees will be led through the process of departure, travel and arrival at the airport to settling in longer-term accommodation.
- *The timing of information provision*: the UK has more control over the quality of information that resettled refugees can receive throughout the resettlement process both prior to and after arrival.
- *The level of choice refugees have about which country to resettle in*: while resettled refugees may arguably have had less choice about which country they will settle in, they may have higher expectations about the destination country than spontaneous asylum seekers.
- *Circumstances prior to arrival*: resettled refugees' may also differ from those of spontaneous asylum seekers. The former may have spent an extensive period of time in a refugee camp. A further distinction may be drawn between those resettled refugees who have been kept in closed camps (who may be particularly vulnerable with greater needs for assistance), compared with those who have been living in open camps.

However, participants noted both resettled refugees and spontaneous refugees have equal rights to protection. Therefore a 'good/bad split' between refugees who have come to the UK on a resettlement programme and those who have come as spontaneous asylum seekers should be avoided. This could also be reflected in equity of the services that they will receive.

Why is information provision important?

Resettled refugees may have been in challenging and uncertain circumstances for a long period of time, with little ability to control or change their circumstances. The provision of information is therefore important to re-empower refugees and to protect people from misinformation and exploitation. Previous experience of resettlement has shown that refugees have a strong desire for information throughout the process. While it may not be possible to prepare someone entirely for the experience of resettlement, the UK may be able to assist refugees with the mental transition through the provision of information.

What are the information needs of resettled refugees pre-departure?

Refugees should be given consistent information at all stages of the resettlement process, including identification, selection, and departure. However, the balance of information should be considered, as too much information pre-departure may result in refugees feeling overloaded with information.

Resettled refugees are likely to need information about the process of resettlement. They may need to know:

- what the criteria are for UK resettlement and how they compare to the criteria of other resettlement countries
- what resettlement the functions of resettlement are and what it does not constitute their chances of selection
- when and how they will be notified if they have been selected

- what their status will be when they arrive in the UK
- what will happen to other family members if the family has been divided
- whether their family member can be resettled as well
- the process upon and after arrival
- what to take to the UK, for example documents such as birth certificates or passports – if they have them.

They could also be given other information about their country of resettlement in the form of cultural orientation. Information could be given on the following topics:

- currency, labour market, and employment possibilities
- education, housing, and transport systems
- government system, and type of government
- history of the UK
- cultural and social norms in the UK
- climate and geography of the UK
- practical tools to assist orientation (such as visits to post offices, supermarkets, health services, etc).

It is important to encourage refugees to have realistic expectations and also prepare them for the reality about the time it may take to find employment, for example. However, it may be difficult to be specific about services because of the variation in local service provision.

When will the information be provided pre-departure?

It takes time to prepare the documentation to resettle someone. This time could be used to plan service and information provision for the refugees. The waiting period before departure could be a wasted opportunity, particularly if it is difficult to predict when refugees will be transported to the UK. During this time, resettled refugees could be given language lessons. However, language provision should not delay departure.

How will the information be presented?

The manner of delivery may be as important or more important than the information itself. Above all, information should be given in a welcoming manner.

A multi-media approach is needed. This would contribute to ensuring that refugees who are illiterate are not excluded. Suggestions for format included a hard copy booklet with visual prompts and videos. These may also be used as complementary tools for language teaching. The benefits of a multi-media approach are that information can be presented to groups, but individuals are also provided with a reference document for future use. Key messages should be reinforced. Information provision should be tailored according to language(s) requirements, and take into account the role of dialects when selecting interpreters.

An awareness of cultural learning patterns and cultural understanding is essential so that information is presented in the most appropriate form. There may be requests for a teacher of a particular gender.

What are the information needs of resettled refugees post-arrival?

Post-arrival, information given may be more specific. Lessons can be learnt from previous and existing programmes. Carrying out individual assessments of need may be very important. A pilot programme was carried out by DWP for refugees living in London. It involved three different stages that were tailored to address each individual's needs. The first stage tackled immediate problems such as social care, health, family reunification, and legal advice. Stage 2 was an individual needs assessment and action plan. Stage 3 assisted people with learning English, provided advice on accessing the labour market and accessing mandatory work programmes e.g. New Deal. By firstly resolving the salient concerns about issues regarding housing and family, refugees could then begin to focus more on employment.

Information could be provided about places where resettled refugees may be able to live more permanently. They could then make an informed choice about where they will live and may be able to visit the area in advance. Another idea was to offer an orientation session to local areas around the reception centre and the longer-term accommodation. Refugees should also be given links to refugee communities and local communities early on.

After resettled refugees have been established in the UK for a period of time, the UK could conduct research with them to learn from their experiences, and their attitudes towards the resettlement experience, and how well they considered their individual needs were addressed.

Who carries out the information provision?

Pre-departure, UK officials and UNHCR representatives could provide the information. Alternatively, information providers could be from the local communities, who are nationals of the refugees' country of origin and who have experience of the refugee process. Currently, information provision is carried out in the US by NGOs and in Europe by central government.

Post-arrival, information provision could be carried out by someone who has local knowledge of the area in which refugees are resettled, who has experience of resettlement and training expertise, and who is from the local community. Refugees themselves could be trained to provide information, or assist with information provision.

Refugees would need to be consulted to find out their views about helping with orientation/information provision.

Information for staff in the UK

Host/reception staff should be provided with specific information regarding individual refugees, their home country, and their circumstances before arriving in the UK. The UNHCR resettlement and integration handbooks are key reference documents, which could be drawn upon during training.

Workshop B

Provision of services, housing, and reception facilities for resettled refugees

Facilitators

Penny Hart (RIU)

Jon Williams (AAPD)

Lesley Duff (IRSS)

Participants

Helen Everett (East Midlands Consortium)

Emma Williams (Medical Foundation for the care of Victims of Torture)

Julia Allen (SRC)

Erik Stenström (Swedish Integration Board)

Van Ly Ung (Refugee Action)

Robin Rennie (East of England Consortium)

Anes Ceric (Refugee UK Network)

Alistair Griggs (Refugee Council)

Wondimu Yohannes (Refugee Action)

Lynnette Kelly (Centre for Research in Ethnic Relations)

Rachel Prime (IRSS)

Deborah Ilott (The Housing Corporation)

Del Jenkins (Jobseeker Analysis Division 6)

Erin Patrick (MPI)

Jim Laird (Scotland Consortium)

Tim Roberts (DoH)

Nev Jefferies (British Red Cross)

Sead Masic (Bosnia Herzegovina Club Ljiljani Northeast)

Paul White (Sheffield University)

Areti Sianni (ECRE London)

Loan Anh Nguyen (Refugee Action)

Miranda Kent (CD)

Nicole Klynman (Médecins Sans Frontières UK)

Sandra Skeete (Refugee Housing Association)

Kate Hitchcock (IRSS)

Laura Turney (Scottish Executive)

Sarah Kincaid (ODPM)

Sanja Potnar (WUS)

Jack Shieh (Vietnamese Mental Health Service)

Patrick Wintour (Employability Forum)

Nadeem Ahmad (North East Consortium)

Jules Harrison (North West Consortium)

Introduction

There are a number of different models of service provision for resettled refugees. The aim of this workshop was to establish what services may be needed for resettled refugees, consider lessons learnt from previous models of service provision, and consider who may be best placed to provide service provision, in order to inform best practice (see Appendix 2 for further information).

What are the service needs of resettled refugees?

Resettled refugees may have mixed and varied needs at different stages of the resettlement process. Consequently, it may be important to carry out an individual and family needs assessment at different stages of the process in order to provide the most appropriate services.

The table below highlights the service needs of refugees post-arrival. While these needs have been broadly arranged according to the time at which they may become a priority, they are all inter-related and each individual refugee may prioritise them differently.

Short-term	Medium-term	Long-term
• refugee status	• training and employment (after assessment)	• citizenship
• basic necessities (such as clothing)	• basic skills training	• participation in society
• links to family members	• re-certification	
• health screening on arrival and health treatment subsequently	• establishing contacts with RCOs, including faith communities, and developing RCO capacity	
• outreach work	• information regarding social context – behaviours, social "norms", laws, childcare issues	
• housing/accommodation in safe place	• community development	
• a welcome and links with existing voluntary networks		
• accessible orientation/information (including transport, shopping etc)		
• interpretation and language provisions (mixed models – classroom does not suit everyone)		
• schooling/education		
• raising awareness with local community		

What best practice is there for receiving, housing, and supporting resettled refugees?

If reception centres are utilised, it may be important to limit the time that resettled refugees will spend in them, to avoid institutionalisation. It may be best to concentrate resources on just a few areas for housing refugees (clustering) in the early stages of the resettlement programme, and try to avoid areas where demand for housing and overcrowding is already high. Informing refugees about locations and providing them with a choice may reduce secondary migration, which is expensive. Providing the opportunity for refugees to visit the potential housing locations first may also assist. Involving refugees in the process of identifying their housing location will help to ensure their involvement in this aspect. The example of the British Red Cross orientation projects was cited as an example.

It will be important to maintain continuity of assistance, from reception centres, through to longer term issues such as schools, housing, jobs, and so on. Those involved in the resettlement process could work in partnership with other agencies by working with refugee communities and a liaison officer. It may be more valuable and effective to work with existing systems and practices, rather than recreating new systems. Some current practice can limit creativity and flexibility with resources. If the system for housing is flexible, the government may be better able to recognise individual and group needs.

Involving existing local and refugee communities, and grass roots RCOs in the resettlement programme is of real importance. Services should try to avoid the "one size fits all" approach and instead focus on meeting individual needs as far as practicable. The government could consider working with local employers to help people find employment. Ideally, service providers would be involved and committed and legal advisors would also be involved.

It may also be useful to involve the media, to try and send out positive messages about resettled refugees, without focusing too heavily on eliciting people's sympathy, which may only be effective in the short term.

Refugees may be lacking in knowledge about services in the UK so there is an ongoing need for information. Information may need to be repeated on an ongoing basis.

It will be important to talk to resettled refugees to find out how they want to engage with the process of service provision as well. It may be easier to manage the expectations of refugees by informing them of what resources are available.

In order to keep identifying best practice, the programme should be evaluated to assess whether the resettlement process and the integration of the resettled refugees have been successful. All those involved in resettlement should continue to share and learn good practice.

Some specific examples of best practice include:

- University of North London – Referral, Advice and Guidance Unit
- Individual primary care projects
- Kosovan HEP programme (for example, in Glasgow).

Workshop C

Alternative models of operating resettlement schemes and the role of resettlement with alternative policy responses

Facilitators

Penny Hart (RIU)

Lesley Duff (IRSS)

Jon Williams (AAPD)

Carolyne Tah (IRSS)

Participants

Furio De Angelis (UNHCR)

Sead Masic (Bosnia Herzegovina Club Ljiljani Northeast)

Wondimu Yohannes (Refugee Action)

Charles Davy (ICMC)

Jules Harrison (North West Consortium)

Nicole Klynman (Médecins Sans Frontières UK)

Joanne van Selm (MPI)

Gil Loescher (IISS)

Liz Westmorland (Yorkshire & Humberside Consortium)

Alistair Griggs (Refugee Council)

Loan Anh Nguyen (Refugee Action)

Patrick Wintour (Employability Forum)

Van Ly Ung (Refugee Action)

Anna Reisenberger (Refugee Council)

Helena Ishmael (Horn of Africa Community Group)

Julia Allen (SRC)

Jan Shaw (Amnesty International)

Deborah Ilott (The Housing Corporation)

Stephanie Dickinson (DWP)

Diane Grammer (IOM)

Jack Shieh (Vietnamese Mental Health Service)

Wondimu Yohannes (Refugee Action)

Kaltun Hassan (RAP)

Rachel Prime (IRSS)

Matthew Gibney (RSC)

Ruben Ahlvin (Swedish Migration Board)

Sandra Skeete (Refugee Housing Association)

Amina Hussein (Red Cross)

Nadeem Ahmad (North East Consortium)

Zamila Bunglawala (Strategic Policy Team)

Lauren Herlitz (IRSS)

Peter Ward (IRSS)

Erik Stenström (Swedish Integration Board)

Vu Khanh Thanh (An Viet Foundation)

Sanja Potnar (WUS)

Sarah Kincaid (ODPM)

Introduction

There are many different ways of processing resettlement cases. The aims of this workshop were to consider how each 'model' for operating resettlement programmes could enhance the UK's ability to provide resettlement and to consider how the quota of refugees will be selected from the number of possible applicants (see Appendix 2 for further information).

Criteria for selection

Countries may use different criteria to select refugees for resettlement. While some countries may use the 1951 Geneva Convention definition, other countries may employ a broader 'Mandate' definition that also identifies refugees who have a continuing need (rather than an immediate need) for protection. Countries may then use further criteria of their own to select their quota of refugees from the vast numbers of refugees in need of protection.

Some participants felt that it was important that the criteria for selection were 'ethically defensible', that is, no refugees should be excluded on the grounds that they may have greater medical needs or would be more difficult to integrate in the UK. Others felt quotas within the quota of 500 could be employed for groups of refugees who may need greater assistance post-arrival.

It was also considered important that the criteria for selection were applied consistently. In order to do so, the UK may need to work closely with UNHCR.

What alternative models are there for resettling refugees?

Mandate scheme

An advantage of this scheme is that it is relatively inexpensive for the government to run. The part of the process currently carried out by the Red Cross was thought to work smoothly. However, if any problems arise in the processing outside of the UK, the Red Cross is responsible for handling complaints. An important disadvantage is that only those refugees who have family in the UK can apply for resettlement.

Dossier selection and interview missions

Dossier selection was considered to be effective for urgent or emergency cases. However, some participants were concerned that there could be higher rejection rates if incomplete application forms were submitted. However, this problem had not arisen in the application forms submitted to the Red Cross for the Mandate scheme.

Interview missions may give the UK a greater level of control over the selection of refugees. UK officials will also be able to see firsthand the circumstances that the refugees are living in. However, UK officials may not be able to access refugees with the greatest needs for protection as they may be risking their own safety. Greater resources are also required. A combination of methods may resolve some of these difficulties, for example, 20 per cent of the quota could be urgent or emergency cases, selected by dossier.

Private sponsorship

Sponsorship may encourage and strengthen wider UK community support and assist community cohesion. It could also have a positive impact on refugee community involvement and support.

Sponsorship could lead to more family reunification. This may present some issues about how the Mandate scheme will fit in with the resettlement programme. Some participants were also concerned that some refugees may be excluded as candidates because they will not have links with potential sponsors. However, they felt that the more refugees that could be protected the better.

Participants raised the point that some people may view private sponsorship sceptically because the government would not have to pay for the refugees' reception and integration. It may therefore be important for the government not to lead private sponsorship schemes directly. Instead, the Home Office could fund the voluntary sector to promote private sponsorship and develop capacity.

Regional resettlement assistance

Many participants felt that it is important to evaluate, develop, and improve the resettlement process to the UK before developing the programme to include resettlement to neighbouring countries in regions of origin. Regional resettlement assistance could be thought of as a complement to the UK resettlement programme and as part of the overall solution for migration management.

Regional resettlement assistance may be effective because refugees could live in a country that has greater cultural or linguistic similarity to their own. Access to relatives may be facilitated and there may be a greater possibility of return to their country of origin. It could also avoid a possible 'brain drain' in their home country and the surrounding regions. Another advantage may be that more refugees could be resettled with public support.

Conversely though, the government may be accused of increasing the burden on other countries by moving the 'problem' elsewhere, and not fulfilling their responsibility for 'burden sharing'.

Resettling to neighbouring regions also relies heavily on other countries agreeing to participate. The government would also have to be certain that the neighbouring regions were secure and stable.

The UK may also have less control over how the money they put into regional resettlement assistance is spent. The UK may need reassurance that the money is being entirely invested into the protection of refugees.

Pre-clearance by NGOs or Overseas Processing Entities (OPEs)

NGOs may want to be involved in the processing of resettlement cases. Their understanding of the experiences of resettled refugees may inform NGOs' involvement at the reception and integration stages of the process. The role of NGOs in the beginning and later stages of the resettlement process could be explored further.

Some participants expressed concern that OPEs can be open to fraud and corruption.

What experience is there of different models for resettlement/supporting refugees in other countries?

Two examples were suggested:

- Referral partners in addition to UNHCR, such as NGOs, could refer cases to the UK and to UNHCR. If a multi-agency approach is adopted, potential delays in case processing may arise. This may be due to the increased number of parties involved. Care would be needed to manage such a system.
- Establishing a process whereby refugees may apply for resettlement at embassies or consulates may provide an alternative avenue to referral and/or resettlement.

Additional best practice suggestions for the UK

These include:

- Learn from the experiences of those who have previously been resettled, particularly with regard to overcoming any feelings of disempowerment that resettled refugees may experience.
- Continue to involve individuals who are knowledgeable about the resettlement process, and who have an international overview of resettlement.
- Involve NGOs in selection missions.

Workshop D

The practicalities of accessing and selecting applicants

Facilitators

Claire Downie (AAPD)   Verity Gelsthorpe (IRSS)

Participants

Erin Patrick (MPI)	James Milner (RSC)	Paul White (Sheffield University)
Anes Ceric (Refugee UK Network)	Lynnette Kelly (Centre for Research in Ethnic Relations)	Nev Jefferies (British Red Cross)
Richard Williams (Refugee Council)	Michael Kingsley-Nynah (UNHCR)	Sarah Hayward (Employability Forum)
Sorcha O'Callaghan (IRC UK)	Patrick Collier (IRSS)	Jim Laird (Scotland Consortium)
Laura Turney (Scottish Executive)	Del Jenkins (Jobseeker Analysis Division 6)	Helen Everett (East Midlands Consortium)
Robin Rennie (East of England Consortium)	Emma Williams (Medical Foundation for the Care of Victims of Torture	Robin Rennie (East of England Consortium)
Tim Roberts (DoH)	Felicity Clarkson (AAPD)	Miranda Kent (CD)
Vaughan Robinson (University of Wales, Swansea)	Kate Hitchcock (IRSS)	

Introduction

Initially, the UK is developing a simple resettlement programme.[67] However, in the future, the programme is likely to develop and may include resettlement for vulnerable groups such as the elderly and unaccompanied minors. The aims of this workshop are to consider the feasibility and practicality of locating vulnerable groups in the field and to consider their particular needs for support and information throughout the resettlement process (see Appendix 2 for more information on aims and UNHCR categories for resettlement).

What are the practical constraints for selecting refugees in at risk groups in the field?

The UK could focus on vulnerable groups by having 'mini' quotas within the overall quota. However, there are a variety of constraints which may impact on selecting any refugees for such mini-quotas in the field. Some of these are specific to identifying refugees from vulnerable groups. They include resource, procedural, and safety constraints. Selection via sub-categories may lead to fraud or corruption, where desperation induces a refugee's claim to be altered to fit in with sub-categories in a quota.

---

67   See AAPD background paper, *UK Quota Resettlement Programme*, Asylum and Appeals Policy Directorate (AAPD), Home Office.

Resource constraints include many general constraints which UNHCR faces. For example, the limited number of spaces available compared to the number of people eligible for resettlement. Additionally, refugee status determination takes approximately ten hours. There is frequently insufficient staffing and there may be a trade-off between quality of case preparation and the quantity of cases because of the lack of resources. Against this, accountability and transparency are needed to avoid subjectivity in selection and corruption in process. It is hard to find examples of how much it costs to resettle vulnerable people (costs are linked to types of post-arrival support to be provided longer term).

Procedural constraints include communication between agencies and within UNHCR which may be slow. There is the time constraint which can lead to an inability to contact an applicant if a missions-based selection system is used. These types of selection missions can also be dependent on the personalities of people on the mission.

Security and physical geography in the field (for example, local conflict, or an inaccessible area) can also affect the ability to identify refugees in certain situations, especially those from vulnerable groups.

Registration

Ideally, information about refugees such as details of family composition, head of household, size of family, and whether applicants have any disabilities would be routinely collated and would assist in the identification of those for resettlement from vulnerable groups. If individuals are not properly registered it may be hard to fill specific or mini-quotas as it may be able to identify who the vulnerable people are. However, there are fundamental problems and difficulties of registration, and a general lack of registration.

Difficulties with registration include:

- Problems in creating and maintaining up-to-date databases. Even some of the most basic details may not be known (for example, the number of family members).
- Problems caused by the flux (both inflows and outflows) of people in camps, which inhibit attempts to register refugees effectively.

By investing in the quality of preparation at registration, information can be provided on the resources and services which will be needed post-arrival, allowing the UK to prepare effectively.

Selection of vulnerable groups

Without adequate registration, other means have to be used to select refugees from vulnerable groups. Although their capacity to operate may be limited, it is possible that NGOs or community groups in the countries of first asylum could be consulted about how to identify vulnerable groups. They could also be involved in making recommendations. However, this may raise concerns about how information would then be managed in the determination process, because problems of measuring vulnerability and potential for fraud could be increased. DFiD could potentially suggest local groups or projects which may be able to assist.

For emergency cases, simple bio-data and reasons why the case is an emergency could be e-mailed to the UK who could make a quick decision. Then, in theory, a full needs assessment could be completed in the field. In reality, this full assessment may be hard to deliver due to limited resources and conflicting, urgent priorities.

How can the UK resettlement programme contribute to international resettlement policy?

The UK programme, although initially limited in size, could be considered as part of the global impact of resettlement on resolving refugee crises, as part of a durable solution. The possibility of whether there is a global refugee situation which could be ameliorated through the joint use of resettlement countries' quotas in a combined resettlement effort, was raised. Taken together and used in a strategic way, they represent a far greater capacity. Some participants felt that the initial UK quota of 500 would make the most valuable contribution by resettling those who were most vulnerable, as it would complement other resettlement countries' selection criteria.

What are needs of vulnerable groups?

Disempowerment may accentuate vulnerability so there is an even greater need to avoid institutionalisation. UK service providers could then go on to develop action plans that address individual needs which are also linked to existing service provision. Some psychological needs may not come to light until after arrival in the UK. Illiteracy may need to be addressed to avoid social exclusion.

Use of resources in the UK

Service provision for vulnerable groups could link into existing services and areas of expertise. This could also reduce the cost of support. Once the services are working successfully, they could then expand and develop.

It may be useful to assess and consider UK expertise and how this might affect the particular contribution that the UK can make to resettlement. For example, the UK could develop expertise in dealing with children and unaccompanied minors.

It is important to recognise that resources are finite, and consider in advance how many resources vulnerable groups of refugees will need.

Panel discussion

Panel Participants:

- Felicity Clarkson
  Director of AAPD
  Home Office

- Vaughan Robinson
  Professor
  University of Swansea, Wales

- Sead Masic
  Representative of Bosnia Herzegovina
  Club Ljiljan Northeast

- Ruben Ahlvin
  Senior Refugee Resettlement Quota
  Co-ordinator Swedish Migration Board

- Joanne van Selm
  Senior Policy Analyst
  Migration Policy Institute

- Gil Loescher
  Senior Fellow for Migration
  International Institute for
  Strategic Studies

- James Milner
  Student Associate
  Refugee Studies Centre
  University of Oxford

- Erik Stenström
  Swedish Integration Board

Q: "What can voluntary organisations do next to move this forward?"

A: *Policy officials*: We will be in contact with NGOs, consortia managers, and local authorities soon to discuss how you can help in the resettlement process. We would like to put across the message that our door is open, and we need you to help us set up and manage the programme.

Sead Masic: RCOs can also play an important role in assisting voluntary and local government organisations with the integration of resettled refugees.

Q: "Given the imminent start of the resettlement programme, what consideration has been given to funding projects that will facilitate resettlement?"

A: *Policy officials*: We have not as yet considered where, or to whom the funding will be allocated for the resettlement programme. The budget for next year has not yet been agreed, but the Home Secretary is committed to the programme. We have budgeted for the fact that we will be supporting people through the first year and for the costs of transporting people here.

> ## Q: "In an age of increased securitisation of immigration law, can we influence the positive profiling of this scheme, and are there any lessons to draw from what we've heard today?"

A: *Ruben Ahlvin*: In Sweden, people do not usually know whether someone is a resettled refugee or another refugee and the programme has full approval from the government. Usually people who know the media say that you cannot control it, however, the British TV, like the Swedish SVT, does have some responsibility, and I think they could do a lot. And Sweden has done that for all refugees by raising awareness of the cultural diversity.

James Milner: The trend of the debate on migration and security in Europe is really focused on 'threats' to European society or national society and culture in some way. I think that resettlement can be portrayed appropriately in the media and can highlight the conditions that refugees face not only from the country of origin but in the country of asylum, and emphasise that refugees are not a source of insecurity but are, in fact, victims of insecurity. I think resettlement can play a very productive role in addressing this perception of asylum seekers as a security threat as a whole.

Joanne van Selm: Broadly speaking, there is quite a positive perception of refugees in the US. Voluntary agencies are very open to talking to the media about refugee groups before they arrive in the United States. There are a lot of profiles on particular groups, for example, in the Sunday newspapers. A past example would be the 'lost boys' of Sudan, and a more recent example is the Somali Bantu where there was a two or three page spread in a newspaper on the situation they fled from, and about the resettlement programme plus pictures. I think this sensitised the public to their situation and prepared the public for their arrival. This could be related to public perception of the Kosovo crisis in the UK, where people saw images of the war. I think it is as important to have that media portrayal before arrival as I think it is to have good relations with the media after arrival. If the Home Office is focusing on particular groups then that is something that the NGOs, for example, could assist with, as they know the regions and know the type of people and know the situations.

Vaughan Robinson: I think we need to explain to the media fully why the policy has been introduced. I think we need to stress that at the core of the policy are protection issues. I agree with you that we need to humanise the policy by challenging stereotypes, and I think we need to educate the public more about the circumstances from which people have come. We need to talk about people before they arrive in the UK and I think we need a medium- to long-term policy as well, in which we continue to talk about the success of policy. We also need to continue to talk about the success of individual refugees as well, so I think a long-term strategy is needed.

> ## Q: "Has there been an optimum size for dispersal or clustering of refugees?"

A: *Vaughan Robinson*: It is a question that has been asked repeatedly, but I do not think researchers have come back with an accurate answer to that. I am not aware of anybody who has ventured that figure in the literature.

Joanne van Selm: I think, as Vaughan said, that nobody would ever come up with the 'optimal' size. I suspect that it depends very much on where the cluster group is being placed, how dispersed the cluster is within the cluster, and where the people come from in the first place and the links that they have, because the aim of clustering is obviously to give support networks. So I think that it probably varies from case to case.

Ruben Ahlvin: In Sweden, we do not have cluster groups at all and we try to disperse refugees as much as we can. I think introducing new groups of refugees are more of an issue for us, rather than the size of the group. However, while new groups may initially appear difficult to integrate, after four or five years people realise they are just like any other group, and the host society and the refugees adapt to each other.

Q: [To Sead Masic] "You mentioned counselling did not work or was not successful, any ideas why?"

A: *Sead Masic*: It is very easy to explain that actually. It did not work because traditionally in some refugees' home countries, counselling does not exist at all. If you would like to tell someone your story it is usually your friend, not even a member of the family but a friend that you can really say everything on your mind to. The organisation's way of counselling was that refugees just talked but counsellors did not. And because refugees talked face-to-face to someone with no answer at all, refugees became suspicious of why the counsellors were just listening to them: *"Why are they doing that?"*, *"Why don't they talk to us?"*, *"Why don't they suggest to us what to do in order to avoid our nightmares?"*. Therefore, after a couple of months, people just said no to counselling and less and less people wanted to attend these sessions. So culturally it was not acceptable, and I believe that they expected a kind of interaction.

Vaughan Robinson: I think there was a recent paper in the British Medical Journal that discussed counselling. It also raised another issue: as counselling can often involve being asked a series of questions, if you are a refugee and you have come from circumstances where being asked questions can determine whether you live or die, it can actually seems a threatening process rather than a healing process.

Sead Masic: Another issue I discovered was that after about four hours on ESOL classes, people did not know what to do with themselves. They were really bored and the rest of the day just walked around. Then we found a couple of training places to keep them occupied. It relieved the pressure so that they did not think about their family members back home all the time and they could actually get on with their lives.

Joanne van Selm: This was brought up at a couple of meetings in the US, where one point that is often raised is that people need to work. And, of course, the US programme is geared towards getting the majority of people working within eight months, and that is seen very much as part of the process of getting over the trauma. But it has also been pointed out that it was as important to give counselling and therapy to deal with the traumas of the resettlement process as it was to deal with the original reason for which there was a protection need.

Participant: There may well be people who have suffered severe trauma who come to the UK on this programme, and I think it would be worthwhile for the government to speak to experts in the Medical Foundation because they have a lot of experience in this field.

Q: "Are reception centres an essential component of UK resettlement policy? If so, how are we going to go about it?"

A: *Policy officials*: We have not yet decided about using reception centres and we will discuss this issue with local government and voluntary and refugee organisations. But a more general question maybe to answer is 'Are reception centres an essential component of a resettlement policy?'.

Ruben Ahlvin: We do not have reception centres for resettled refugees at all and there is no clustering of any kind. Their individual accommodation is arranged for them – maybe a flat in a city or in a small village – and they go directly there. Reception centres are only for asylum seekers during their asylum procedure in Sweden. Some secondary migration to the major cities does occur. In the small cities, local government staff give refugees an introduction to the area.

Erik Stenström: When they are accepted within the quota if they have relatives in Sweden we try to find the same location for the newcomer, but otherwise we decide where they will settle.

Sead Masic: During the Bosnian experience the reception centre was an option and it did benefit the refugees. But the way the newspapers actually write about the refugees today, I would not think that would be the ideal option right now. The reception centre was also a community centre. There were so many people from the same country and they really understood all the cultural differences between themselves and the host community. But it may be a different experience if different communities are under one roof and have to share everything.

Joanne van Selm: The current system in the Netherlands, since 1999 when the centre which was specifically for the invited or resettled refugees was closed, is that resettled refugees go into the asylum seekers centre. That means that they are mixed in with people who are waiting for status determination and people who have refugee status but are still waiting for housing (which can be for up to 18 months). The results do not look very good. In fact most of the people who work with the refugees say that the previous system of a dedicated centre for resettled refugees worked far better because it was far more geared to their particular needs.

In the United States there are no reception centres at all. People who have family, even extended family in the country, whether they are coming for the family link or not, are placed in the same state and preferably in the same city, so that they are close to that family member. They are dependent on a voluntary agency finding housing for them, or family members finding housing for them.

In Canada, the privately sponsored refugees go directly into housing which their sponsor organises. There is not a reception facility for them. But government-assisted refugees, generally speaking, go into a reception centre for about three weeks on arrival. These are run by NGOs, and they are primarily for the resettled refugees. If there is space left open at a particular point in the year because there have not been so many arrivals, then the space that is available will be used if necessary for any asylum seekers or immigrants who are homeless. They never stay in the centre for more than three weeks, as housing becomes available. During the three-week period, they will be shown how to go to the supermarket, how to use transport, and they try to make sure that the housing for them is within an hour-and-a-half to two-hour radius away from the centre. The centre serves as a community centre in a sense as well and they can always come back there. One reception centre in Vancouver was a particularly interesting example where the reception facilities were independent housing units, like little apartments, and they had about seventy beds or so, built above the offices of the NGO. The NGO group which was providing the information about available services in Vancouver and British Columbia, was right downstairs so that any moment when people felt that they needed to talk, or they needed information on something, they could just go downstairs and ask for it.

Vaughan Robinson: My personal view is that short-term residence in hostels or whatever category of reception centre is a good thing for a number of reasons. I think they act in effect as a 'decompression chamber' and they allow people temporary sanctuary to adjust to new circumstances in an unthreatening environment. I think if they are sited in appropriate places within resettlement areas they can act as a community resource and they can allow settled refugees to contribute to the reception and resettlement of the next group. I think they also offer an opportunity to collect or assess information about the needs of individuals in a non-threatening environment, and I think they are also an efficient way of providing services such as orientation services professionally and cost effectively.

Appendices

Appendix 1:   Seminar programme

9:00–9:30   Registration and coffee

9:30–9:45   Open and welcome – The Home Office and resettlement: background to UK resettlement policy development and research activities – working assumptions for policy development and current research needs and questions
Ms. Felicity Clarkson, Director, Asylum and Appeals Policy Directorate, Home Office

9:45–10:15   Presentation 1: Lessons from the past and considerations for the new programme
Vaughan Robinson, Professor, University of Swansea

10:15–10:40   Presentation 2: The experience of resettlement
Mr. Sead Masic, Representative of Bosnia Herzegovina Club Ljiljan Northeast

10:40–11:00   Presentation 3: Best practice and lessons learned for integration following the resettlement integration conference
Mr. Ruben Ahlvin, Senior Refugee Resettlment Quota Co-ordinator, Swedish Migration Board and Mr. Erik Stenström, Swedish Integration Board

11:00–11:15   Morning coffee

11:15–12:30   Morning workshops: Preparing for the UK resettlement scheme
Group A) Information needs of resettled refugees pre-departure and post-arrival
Group B) Provision of services, housing and reception facilities for resettled refugees

12:30–13:30   Lunch

13:30–13:50   Presentation 4: Key lessons for the UK from the USA and Canada.
Dr Joanne van Selm, Senior Policy Analyst, Migration Policy Institute, Washington

13:50–14:10   Presentation 5: Conditions and constraints of resettlement activities in the regions of origin, with particular reference to Turkey, the Middle East and East Africa
Professor Gil Loescher, Senior Fellow for Migration, Forced Displacement and International Security, International Institute for Strategic Studies

14:10–14:30   Presentation 6: Implications of recent developments in international resettlement policy for UK resettlement policy
Mr. James Milner, Student Associate, Refugee Studies Centre, University of Oxford

14:30–15.45   Afternoon workshops: Development of the UK progamme beyond 2003
Group C) Alternative models of operating resettlement schemes and the role of resettlement with alternative policy responses
Group D) The practicalities of accessing and selecting applicants

15:45–16.00   Afternoon coffee

16:00–16.45   Panel discussion and feedback session
               Chair: Ms. Felicity Clarkson, AAPD
               Professor Vaughan Robinson, University of Swansea
               Mr. Sead Masic, Representative of Bosnia Herzegovina Club Ljiljan Northeast
               Mr. Ruben Ahlvin, Senior Refugee Resettlment Quota Co-ordinator, Swedish Migration Board
               Mr. Erik Stenström, Swedish Integration Board
               Dr Joanne van Selm, Senior Policy Analyst, Migration Policy Institute, Washington
               Prof. Gil Loescher, Senior Fellow for Migration, Forced Displacement and International Security, International Institute for Strategic Studies
               Mr. James Milner, Student Associate, Refugee Studies Centre, University of Oxford

16:45–17:00   Close

Appendix 2: Workshop questions

Morning workshop sessions: preparing for the UK resettlement scheme

Group A) Information needs of resettled refugees pre-departure and post-arrival

A variety of information can be provided to resettled refugees at various stages of the resettlement process. This can cover many aspects of resettlement such as information about the process itself, preparation for departure, and orientation for arrival and longer-term integration.

Aims

- To establish what the information needs of resettled refugees are, both pre-departure and post-arrival.
- To share learning and best practice about these information needs from previous resettlement programmes and those taking place elsewhere.

Key questions

- What practical information do resettled refugees need?
- Does experience point to resettled refugees needing additional or different support to spontaneous refugees post-arrival? If so, what are the differences and how are these addressed in information provision?
- What has been achieved through the provision of information or orientation advice before departure: can anything prepare refugees for arriving in the UK?
- Have we sought in the past to provide cultural information about life in the UK? How did this work?
- Are there lessons we can learn from work on citizenship, or refugee integration: does experience with resettled refugees point to these needing to be tailored or altered in any way?
- What measures can be taken to address barriers to integration in pre-departure and post-arrival assistance?

Group B) Provision of services, housing and reception facilities for resettled refugees

There are a number of different models for receiving, housing, and providing services to resettled refugees. These include reception centres, permanent housing, and clustered, self-contained accommodation.

Aims

- To establish what the service provision needs of resettled refugees are, who is best placed to provide them, and what the service provider(s) need(s) in order to be able to carry this out.
- To establish which models of service provision worked in previous resettlement programmes and which did not, and to consider which changes are necessary in order to improve them.

Key questions

- What are the service needs of resettled refugees? E.g. health screening, employment assistance, accommodation provision, access to education, and language training.
- Who should/would want to provide the assistance? Central government, local government, NGOs, volunteers?
- What assistance and information do other actors require to deliver this?
- What links do there need to be between actors in order to achieve this?
- What best practice is there for receiving, housing, and supporting resettled refugees?
- What does experience suggest that would enable us to make optimum use of resources?

Afternoon workshop sessions: development of the UK programme beyond 2003

Group C) Alternative models of operating resettlement schemes and the role of resettlement with alternative policy responses

Resettlement is the most expensive way to provide protection to refugees. There are various ways of processing resettlement cases and operating a resettlement programme. These include the use of 'overseas processing entities' (OPEs) for case preparation, private sponsorship schemes, dossier selection, interview missions, or resettlement to neighbouring regions.

Aim

- To consider the role of the various 'models' for operating resettlement programmes, and how these might be implemented in the UK to enhance our ability to provide resettlement.

Key questions

- What would the benefits be for resettlement to the UK of dossier selection, or using an OPE? What would we need to do so that these methods – or others – could work here?
- The UK already has a form of sponsorship for resettlement to the UK in the mandate refugee scheme where families support those arriving. What would the considerations be if a wider sponsorship programme were to be introduced?
- What experience is there of different models for resettlement or supporting refugees in other countries?
- What are their advantages, constraints, and drawbacks?
- What would they achieve?
- Does experience suggest that they could work in the UK?
- How?

Overseas Processing Entity (OPE): Cases referred to the USA are first processed by an OPE to verify the quality of documentation and conduct necessary checks. The US Government makes final decisions for each case. For countries with a large quota, this investment of resources enables the state to find and consider more cases for resettlement each year, thereby meeting its target.

Private sponsorship schemes: These enable resettlement states to increase their capacity, as the sponsoring group funds the resettlement and makes provision for the refugee's integration. In some cases private sponsorship is limited to families of the refugee (similar to the Mandate Refugee Scheme) but in other states faith groups, community organisations, and private individuals may also sponsor a refugee's resettlement. There are generally strict rules and obligations regarding sponsorship and screening is conducted to ensure that the sponsoring body is appropriate.

Dossier selection: Some states accept resettlement cases on the basis of paper dossiers without interviewing the applicant themselves. The impact of this has been mixed: it can speed up the rate of resettlement, radically reducing the time taken to consider cases; but can also lead to higher rejection rates for cases, sometimes simply because insufficient information is provided.

Alternatives to resettlement: Alternatives to resettlement include funding resettlement to neighbouring countries (for example, Sweden funds the resettlement of Colombians to other countries in South America); and Australia provides a visa application channel for asylum seekers.

Group D) The practicalities of accessing and selecting applicants

For the first year of the resettlement programme, the intention is to begin with a simple scheme. In the future it is likely that the programme will develop to resettle groups like unaccompanied children, women at risk, or people with greater medical needs.

Aims

- To find out what best practice and experience tells us about how to locate refugees for resettlement from vulnerable groups, given operating constraints in the field.
- To establish if experience shows that these refugees need different (or extra) support or information during the resettlement process, and post-arrival in the UK.

Key questions

- How practical is selection using sub-categories or at-risk groups such as medical cases, women at risk, unaccompanied minors?
- What are the priority areas of international resettlement policy that should be incorporated into UK resettlement policy? For example, priority criteria and procedures for vulnerable groups, resettlement as a tool of protection for individual refugees versus an expression of international solidarity with host countries?
- What are the practical constraints for selecting refugees in these categories?
- Considerations and requirements for assistance: from experience with working with refugees and asylum seekers or other evidence, what extra considerations need to be made regarding these groups?
- What extra/different services or support would they need?
- Would resettling some categories place too much pressure on resources?

It is possible that the increased costs associated with resettling a large number of refugees who would have higher than usual resource needs may necessitate a reduction in the quota to reflect a higher cost per person.

UNHCR's categories for resettlement are:

- legal and physical protection needs;
- survivors of violence and torture;
- medical needs;
- women at risk;
- family reunification;
- children and adolescents;
- elderly refugees; and
- refugees without local integration prospects.

Appendix 3:   List of Participants

Ruben Ahlvin, Swedish Migration Board

Nadeem Ahmad, North East Consortium

Julia Allen, Scottish Refugee Council

Furio De Angelis, UNHCR

Zamila Bunglawala, Strategic Policy Team, Home Office

Anes Ceric, Refugee UK Network

Felicity Clarkson, AAPD, Home Office

Patrick Collier, IRSS, Home Office

Ralph Clarkson, IRSS, Home Office

Charles Davy, ICMC

Stephanie Dickinson, DWP

Claire Downie, AAPD, Home Office

Lesley Duff, IRSS, Home Office

Helen Everett, East Midlands Consortium

Verity Gelsthorpe, IRSS, Home Office

Matthew Gibney, RSC, University of Oxford

Diane Grammer, IOM

Alistair Griggs, Refugee Council

Jules Harrison, North West Consortium

Penny Hart, RIU, Home Office

Kaltun Hassan, RAP

Sarah Hayward, Employability Forum

Lauren Herlitz, IRSS, Home Office

Kate Hitchcock, IRSS, Home Office

Amina Hussein Red Cross

Deborah Ilott, The Housing Corporation

Helena Ishmael, Horn of Africa Community Group

Nev Jefferies, British Red Cross

Del Jenkins, Jobseeker Analysis Division 6

Lynnette Kelly, Centre for Research in Ethnic Relations, University of Warwick

Miranda Kent, Communications Directorate, Home Office

Michael Kingsley-Nynah, UNHCR UK

Sarah Kincaid, ODPM, Homelessness Directorate

Nicole Klynman, Médecins Sans Frontières UK

Jim Laird, Scotland Consortium

Gil Loescher, IISS

Beverley Martin-Mayo, IRSS, Home Office

Sead Masic, Bosnia Herzegovina Club Ljiljani Northeast

James Milner, RSC, University of Oxford

Loan Anh Nguyen, Refugee Action

Sorcha O'Callaghan, IRC UK

Erin Patrick, MPI

Sanja Potnar, WUS

Rachel Prime, IRSS, Home Office

Anna Reisenberger, Refugee Council

Robin Rennie, East of England Consortium

Tim Roberts, DoH

Vaughan Robinson, University of Wales, Swansea

Joanne van Selm, MPI

Jan Shaw, Amnesty International

Jack Shieh, Vietnamese Mental Health Service

Areti Sianni, ECRE London

Sandra Skeete, Refugee Housing Association

Erik Stenström, Swedish Integration Board

Carolyne Tah, IRSS, Home Office

Vu Khanh Thanh, An Viet Foundation

Laura Turney, Scottish Executive Social Justice (Equalities) Research Team

Van Ly Ung, Refugee Action

Peter Ward, IRSS, Home Office

Liz Westmorland, Yorkshire & Humberside Consortium

Paul White, Department of Geography, Sheffield University

Emma Williams, Medical Foundation for the care of Victims of Torture

Jon Williams, IAPU, Home Office

Richard Williams, Refugee Council

Patrick Wintour, Employability Forum

Wondimu Yohannes, Refugee Action

Appendix 4:   Evaluation form

Please take a few minutes to answer the questions below by ticking the appropriate boxes/circles and writing in your comments.

---

1. Regarding your work with refugees and resettlement, how valuable has the conference been for you overall?

○ Very valuable   ○ Quite valuable   ○ Not very valuable   ○ Not at all valuable

2. What was the most valuable aspect or outcome of the seminar for you? (Write in)

....

3. In your view, in what way, if any, did the seminar fail to fulfil its potential? (Write in)

....

The aims of this seminar were to inform current policy development and implementation of the forthcoming UK resettlement programme, and to inform future strategic policy development of the UK resettlement programme by developing an evidence and research base.

4. How relevant were the aims of the seminar to your work?

○ Very relevant   ○ Quite relevant   ○ Not very relevant   ○ Not at all relevant

5. How successful was the seminar in achieving each of the following aims?

	Very successful	Quite successful	Not very successful	Not at all successful
Sharing existing research evidence, knowledge, experience, ideas, and examples of good practices on resettlement	❏	❏	❏	❏
Facilitating information-sharing about lessons learnt from past UK experience of resettlement programmes	❏	❏	❏	❏
Facilitating information-sharing about gaps in current knowledge and research evidence	❏	❏	❏	❏

6. How valuable did you consider each of the following aspects of the day to be?

	Very valuable	Quite valuable	Not very valuable	Not at all valuable
Presentations from researchers, officials, and refugee community representative	❏	❏	❏	❏
Workshops	❏	❏	❏	❏
Closing plenary session	❏	❏	❏	❏
Networking opportunities throughout the day	❏	❏	❏	❏

7. How relevant to your work were the topic areas that were covered in the workshops?

○ Very relevant   ○ Quite relevant   ○ Not very relevant   ○ Not at all relevant

8. If there was a topic that was not covered in the workshops that you feel should have been, please write in what this was.

....

9. How would you rate each of the following organisational aspects of the seminar?

	Very good	Quite good	Adequate	Quite poor	Very poor
Administration prior to the event	❏	❏	❏	❏	❏
Organisation during the event	❏	❏	❏	❏	❏
The venue and its facilities	❏	❏	❏	❏	❏
Lunch and refreshments during the day	❏	❏	❏	❏	❏
Seminar pack materials	❏	❏	❏	❏	❏

10. Any other comments you have would be very welcome. Please write them here.

....

....

....

11. What is your organisation/role?

○ UK academic   ○ IND   ○ Other government   ○ NGO

○ Non-UK academic   ○ Other Home Office   ○ Government (non-UK) ○ Other (write in)

....

Your name (feel free to leave this blank) ....

THANK YOU FOR YOUR TIME. PLEASE PUT THIS FORM IN THE BASKETS PROVIDED BEFORE YOU LEAVE THE SEMINAR.